Index

1. Introduction to Clinical Pharmacokinetics

- Clinical pharmacokinetics is a branch of pharmacology dedicated to the study of the time course of drug absorption, distribution, metabolism, and excretion (ADME) in the human body, with the goal of optimizing drug therapy in individual patients.
- It combines pharmacokinetics (PK) with clinical practice to ensure the safe, effective, and personalized use of medications.

Definition of Pharmacokinetics

- Pharmacokinetics literally means "what the body does to the drug."
- It is concerned with the quantitative analysis of how drugs move through the body and includes the following key processes:
  - ➢ **Absorption:** The movement of a drug from the site of administration into the bloodstream.
  - ➢ **Distribution:** The dispersion or dissemination of substances throughout the fluids and tissues of the body.
  - ➢ **Metabolism (Biotransformation):** The chemical alteration of the drug by the body, mainly in the liver.
  - ➢ **Excretion:** The removal of the substances from the body, primarily via the kidneys (urine) or through bile (faeces).

The acronym **ADME** is commonly used to summarize these four processes.

Types of Order in Pharmacokinetics

- Pharmacokinetics involves the study of the rate at which drugs move through the body.
- This movement can follow different kinetic orders, primarily:
  - Zero-Order Kinetics
  - First-Order Kinetics
  - Mixed-Order (Nonlinear) Kinetics or Michaelis-Menten Kinetics
- Each of these has different implications for drug dosing, therapeutic monitoring, and potential for toxicity.

First-Order Kinetics (Linear Kinetics)

- In first-order kinetics, the rate of drug elimination is directly proportional to the concentration of the drug in the body.
- This is the most common kinetic order for most drugs at therapeutic doses.

Key Characteristics

- A constant fraction or percentage of the drug is eliminated per unit time.
- The elimination rate increases as drug concentration increases.
- The half-life ($t^{1/2}$) is constant, regardless of drug concentration.
- The rate equation is:

$$dc/dt = -kC$$

Where *C* is the drug concentration and *k* is the first-order elimination rate constant.

Clinical Implications

- Predictable pharmacokinetics.
- Dose adjustments are straightforward.
- Most drugs like paracetamol, amoxicillin, and atenolol follow first-order kinetics.

Zero-Order Kinetics (Non-Linear Kinetics at High Dose)

- In zero-order kinetics, the rate of drug elimination is constant and independent of the drug concentration.
- This occurs when the eliminating enzymes or pathways are saturated.

Key Characteristics

- A constant amount of drug is eliminated per unit time, regardless of plasma concentration.
- The half-life is not constant and can vary with concentration.
- The rate equation is:

$$dc/dt = -k$$

Where k is the zero-order rate constant.

Examples

- Phenytoin
- Ethanol (alcohol)
- Aspirin at high doses

Clinical Implications

- Small changes in dose can lead to large changes in plasma concentration.
- Higher risk of accumulation and toxicity.
- Requires careful monitoring and individualized dosing.

Mixed-Order (Nonlinear or Michaelis-Menten) Kinetics

- Some drugs exhibit mixed-order kinetics, where the drug initially follows first-order kinetics, but at higher concentrations, the metabolic pathways become saturated and the drug switches to zero-order kinetics.

Key Characteristics

- At low concentrations: First-order elimination.
- At high concentrations: Zero-order elimination due to enzyme saturation.
- Based on Michaelis-Menten equation:

$$\frac{dC}{dt} = \frac{V_{max} \cdot C}{K_m + C}$$

Where:

- Vmax: Maximum rate of elimination
- Km: Drug concentration at half of Vmax
- C: Plasma concentration

Examples

- Phenytoin: Widely known for its mixed-order kinetics.
- Theophylline
- Warfarin at high doses

Clinical Implications

- Dose increases may cause disproportionate rises in plasma levels.
- Risk of toxicity increases significantly once enzyme systems are saturated.
- Requires therapeutic drug monitoring (TDM).

Feature	First-Order Kinetics	Zero-Order Kinetics	Mixed-Order Kinetics
Elimination rate	Proportional to drug conc.	Constant (enzyme saturated)	Changes from 1st to 0-order
Amount eliminated/time	Varies	Constant	Varies
Half-life (t½)	Constant	Not constant	Not constant
Common examples	Most drugs	Ethanol, phenytoin (high)	Phenytoin, theophylline
Clinical management	Predictable	Risk of toxicity	Requires close monitoring

Understanding the order of pharmacokinetics is essential for:

- Designing accurate dosage regimens.
- Preventing drug accumulation and toxicity.
- Managing patient-specific therapy, especially in high-risk or critical care settings.
- Drugs following first-order kinetics are generally easier to manage, while zero-order and nonlinear kinetics demand more precise dosing and monitoring.

Clinical Pharmacokinetics

- Clinical pharmacokinetics applies the principles of pharmacokinetics to the safe and effective therapeutic management of drugs in patients.
- It involves adjusting drug dosage regimens based on individual patient characteristics to achieve optimal therapeutic outcomes with minimal toxicity.
- It bridges the gap between laboratory pharmacokinetics and patient care by focusing on:
  - Individual variability in drug response
  - Disease impact on drug handling
  - Drug interactions
  - Special populations (e.g., paediatrics, geriatrics, renal or hepatic impairment)

Pharmacokinetic Parameters

- Several important parameters are used in clinical pharmacokinetics to describe and predict drug behaviour:
  - **Bioavailability (F):** The fraction of the administered dose that reaches systemic circulation in an unchanged form.
  - **Volume of Distribution (V_d):** A hypothetical volume that relates the amount of drug in the body to the plasma concentration.
  - **Clearance (Cl):** The rate at which the drug is eliminated from the body.
  - **Half-life ($t^{1/2}$):** The time required for the plasma concentration of a drug to reduce by half.
  - **Peak concentration (Cmax) and Time to peak (Tmax):** Important for assessing drug efficacy and toxicity.
- Understanding these parameters allows clinicians to predict drug concentrations over time and adjust dosing accordingly.

Importance of Clinical Pharmacokinetics in Therapy

- **Personalized Medicine:** Tailoring drug regimens based on the patient's pharmacokinetic profile helps enhance therapeutic efficacy and minimize side effects.
- **Therapeutic Drug Monitoring (TDM):** Measurement of drug concentrations in the blood to maintain a constant therapeutic level.
- **Dose Adjustment:** Especially critical in patients with altered physiology (e.g., renal or hepatic dysfunction).
- **Managing Drug Interactions:** Identifying and managing PK interactions that can lead to reduced efficacy or increased toxicity.
- **Improving Outcomes:** Appropriate dosing leads to improved clinical outcomes and reduced hospital stays and costs.

Factors Affecting Pharmacokinetics in Clinical Settings

- A wide range of patient-specific and drug-specific factors can influence pharmacokinetics:
  - **Age:** Neonates and the elderly may have reduced metabolism and clearance.
  - **Body weight and composition:** Obesity or cachexia can alter distribution and metabolism.
  - **Genetic factors:** Polymorphisms in drug-metabolizing enzymes (e.g., CYP450 enzymes).
  - **Organ function:** Hepatic and renal impairment can significantly affect drug clearance.
  - **Drug formulation:** Modified-release or enteric-coated forms can alter absorption.
  - **Route of administration:** Oral, intravenous, transdermal, etc., affect bioavailability and onset of action.

Applications of Clinical Pharmacokinetics

- Clinical pharmacokinetics is widely used in:
  - Hospital pharmacy practice
  - Drug development and clinical trials
  - Critical care and oncology
  - Infectious disease treatment (e.g., antibiotics)
  - Chronic disease management (e.g., epilepsy, cardiovascular diseases)

Challenges in Clinical Pharmacokinetics

- While extremely useful, clinical pharmacokinetics faces some challenges:
  - Variability in patient compliance and lifestyle

- ➢ Limited access to timely and accurate drug concentration data
- ➢ Complexities of polypharmacy in chronic diseases
- ➢ Difficulty in interpreting PK data in special populations

- Clinical pharmacokinetics plays a pivotal role in modern therapeutics by integrating drug concentration data with individual patient variables to optimize drug therapy.
- As the field of personalized medicine continues to grow, the importance of clinical pharmacokinetics in delivering tailored, effective, and safe treatments is expected to become even more prominent.

Parameter	Definition	Clinical Importance
Bioavailability (F)	Fraction of drug reaching systemic circulation after administration	Determines dose needed to achieve therapeutic effect; affected by first-pass metabolism
Volume of Distribution (V_d)	Apparent volume in which a drug is distributed	Indicates how widely a drug spreads in body tissues
Clearance (Cl)	Volume of plasma cleared of drug per unit time	Determines the rate of drug elimination; used to calculate maintenance dose
Half-life (t ½)	Time for drug concentration to fall by 50%	Used to determine dosing interval and time to reach steady state
Peak concentration (C_{max})	Maximum plasma concentration of a drug	Helps predict efficacy and risk of toxicity
Time to peak (T_{max})	Time to reach Cmax	Important in evaluating onset of drug action
Area under the curve (AUC)	Total drug exposure over time	Reflects overall drug exposure; used to compare bioavailability

2. Design of Dosage Regimens

Introduction

- A **dosage regimen** refers to the **schedule and amount of drug administration** designed to achieve and maintain a desired **therapeutic concentration** of a drug in the body over a period of time.
- The goal is to ensure **efficacy** while **minimizing toxicity**.
- Designing a dosage regimen involves integrating pharmacokinetic principles with patient-specific factors to provide **optimal therapeutic benefit**.

Objectives of Dosage Regimen Design

- **Achieve therapeutic drug levels quickly (without toxicity)**
- **Maintain steady-state concentration (Css) within the therapeutic window**
- **Avoid sub-therapeutic or toxic concentrations**
- **Account for patient variability (age, weight, renal/hepatic function)**
- **Minimize dosing frequency to improve compliance**

Key Pharmacokinetic Concepts in Dosage Design

- To design an effective dosage regimen, the following pharmacokinetic parameters are essential:

Parameter	Function
Clearance (Cl)	Determines maintenance dose to maintain steady-state levels
Volume of Distribution (Vd)	Influences loading dose required to rapidly achieve Css
Half-life ($t_{1/2}$)	Guides dosing interval and time to reach steady-state
Bioavailability (F)	Affects the actual dose needed when not given intravenously
Therapeutic Window	Range between minimum effective and toxic concentrations

Components of a Dosage Regimen

- A dosage regimen typically includes:
    - **Loading Dose (LD)**
    - **Maintenance Dose (MD)**
    - **Dosing Interval (τ)**

Loading Dose (LD)

- A **loading dose** is an initial higher dose of a drug that may be given at the beginning of a treatment to quickly achieve a therapeutic concentration.

$$\text{Loading Dose} = \frac{C_{\text{target}} \times V_d}{F}$$

Where:

- Ctarget: Desired plasma concentration
- Vd: Volume of distribution
- F: Bioavailability

- Used for drugs with **long half-lives** to rapidly reach therapeutic levels (e.g., digoxin, amiodarone).

Maintenance Dose (MD)

- A **maintenance dose** is the amount of drug given repeatedly to maintain a steady-state concentration within the therapeutic range.

$$\text{Maintenance Dose} = \frac{C_{\text{ss}} \times Cl \times \tau}{F}$$

Where:

- Css: Desired steady-state concentration, Cl: Clearance, τ\tau: Dosing interval, F: Bioavailability

Dosing Interval (τ)

- The **dosing interval** is the time between each dose administration.
  - Based on the **half-life** of the drug.
  - Drugs with short half-lives may require **frequent dosing**.
  - Drugs with long half-lives can be dosed **less frequently**.

Types of Dosage Regimens

A. Fixed-Dose Regimen (Multiple Dosing): Regular doses at fixed intervals and most common form in clinical practice.

B. Variable-Dose Regimen: Dose adjusted based on patient response (e.g., insulin, warfarin).

C. Continuous Infusion: Used to maintain **constant plasma concentrations** and common in ICU settings (e.g., dopamine, nitroglycerin).

D. Intermittent Dosing: Doses are spaced apart to allow drug levels to drop between doses and useful in minimizing side effects (e.g., chemotherapy).

Factors Affecting Dosage Regimen Design

Patient Factors

- Age (e.g., neonates, geriatrics)
- Body weight and surface area
- Renal and hepatic function
- Genetic polymorphisms
- Comorbidities

Drug Factors

- Route of administration
- Half-life
- Bioavailability
- Therapeutic index (narrow or wide)
- Drug interactions

Therapeutic Considerations

- Onset and duration of action required
- Need for rapid therapeutic effect
- Risk of toxicity
- Adherence potential

Steady-State and Time to Reach Steady-State

- **Steady-state concentration (Css)** is reached when **rate of drug administration = rate of elimination**.
- It typically takes **4–5 half-lives** to reach steady-state with regular dosing.
- Using a **loading dose** can shorten the time to reach Css.

Example: Designing a Dosage Regimen

Let's say:

- Desired Css = 10 mg/L
- Clearance (Cl) = 5 L/h
- Bioavailability (F) = 0.8
- Dosing interval (τ) = 12 hours

Maintenance Dose

$$MD = \frac{10 \times 5 \times 12}{0.8} = \frac{600}{0.8} = 750 \text{ mg}$$

So, **750 mg every 12 hours** maintains the target Css.

- Designing dosage regimens is a fundamental aspect of clinical pharmacokinetics and personalized medicine. A well-designed regimen ensures:
    - **Therapeutic effectiveness**
    - **Minimal toxicity**
    - **Improved patient adherence**
- By carefully considering pharmacokinetic parameters and patient-specific variables, healthcare professionals can tailor dosing strategies that maximize benefit and minimize risk.

Nomograms and Tabulations in Designing Dosage Regimens

- In clinical pharmacokinetics, **nomograms and tabulations** are practical tools used to **simplify the design of dosage regimens**.
- They allow healthcare professionals to **quickly estimate loading doses, maintenance doses, and dosing intervals** without performing complex mathematical calculations manually.
- These tools are especially valuable in time-sensitive clinical settings such as **intensive care units, emergency rooms**, and during **therapeutic drug monitoring**.

Nomograms

- A **nomogram** is a **graphical calculating tool** that consists of a chart or diagram with multiple scales representing different pharmacokinetic variables.
- By aligning a straight line across known values (such as patient weight, drug clearance, or desired concentration), clinicians can quickly find unknown variables like **dosing amounts** or **drug concentrations**.

Types of Nomograms Used in Pharmacokinetics

Nomogram Type	Purpose
Loading dose nomogram	Calculate the initial dose required to reach therapeutic level
Maintenance dose nomogram	Estimate the ongoing dose to maintain steady-state levels
Vancomycin/aminoglycoside nomograms	Estimate dose and interval based on weight and creatinine clearance
Phenytoin nomogram	Adjust dose in nonlinear kinetics
Theophylline nomogram	Used for drugs with narrow therapeutic windows

TABLE 1: Bolus Dose

WEIGHT (kg)	RISK OF BLEEDING			
	LOW RISK		RAISED RISK	
	Bolus (units)	*Bolus (mLs)*	*Bolus (units)*	*Bolus (mLs)*
45-49	3600	**0.72**	2700	**0.5**
50-54	4000	**0.8**	3000	**0.6**
55-59	4400	**0.9**	3300	**0.7**
60-64	4800	**1**	3600	**0.7**
65-69	5200	**1**	3900	**0.8**
70-74	5600	**1.1**	4200	**0.8**
75-79	6000	**1.2**	4500	**0.9**
80-84	6400	**1.3**	4800	**1**
85-89	6800	**1.4**	5000	**1**
90-94	7200	**1.5**	5000	**1**
95-99	7600	**1.5**	5000	**1**
100-104	8000	**1.6**	5000	**1**
105-109	8400	**1.7**	5000	**1**
110-114	8800	**1.8**	5000	**1**
115-119	9200	**1.8**	5000	**1**
≥120	9600	**1.9**	5000	**1**

TABLE 2: Initial Infusion Rate

WEIGHT (kg)	RISK OF BLEEDING			
	LOW RISK		RAISED RISK	
	Rate (units/hr)	*Rate (mLs/hr)*	*Rate (units/hr)*	*Rate (mLs/hr)*
45-49	800	**1.6**	540	**1.1**
50-54	900	**1.8**	600	**1.2**
55-59	1000	**2**	660	**1.3**
60-64	1100	**2.2**	720	**1.4**
65-69	1200	**2.4**	780	**1.6**
70-74	1300	**2.6**	840	**1.7**
75-79	1400	**2.8**	900	**1.8**
80-84	1500	**3**	960	**1.9**
85-89	1600	**3.2**	1000	**2**
90-94	1700	**3.4**	1000	**2**
95-99	1700	**3.4**	1000	**2**
100-104	1800	**3.6**	1000	**2**
105-109	1900	**3.8**	1000	**2**
110-114	2000	**4**	1000	**2**
115-119	2100	**4.2**	1000	**2**

TABLE 3: Infusion Adjustment

APTT (seconds)	Additional Action	Infusion Rate Adjustment
<30	Repeat Bolus Dose from **Table 1**	**Increase** by 0.4 mL/hr
30-39	None	**Increase** by 0.2 mL/hr
40-49	None	**Increase** by 0.1 mL/hr
50-75	None	No change: *in therapeutic range*
76-90	None	**Decrease** by 0.2 mL/hr
91-110	**STOP** infusion for 1 hour	**Decrease** by 0.4 mL/hr when restarting
>110	**STOP** infusion for 2 hours	**Decrease** by 0.6 mL/hr when restarting
Inform doctor if APTT > 110 for TWO consecutive readings		

Advantages of Nomograms

- Quick and easy to use at bedside
- Require minimal calculation
- Ideal for initial dose estimation in acute settings
- Helps visualize pharmacokinetic relationships

Example: Vancomycin Nomogram

- A vancomycin dosing nomogram may use:
  - **Patient's weight (kg)**
  - **Creatinine clearance (CrCl, mL/min)**
  - **Target trough level (e.g., 15–20 µg/mL)**
- By aligning these variables, clinicians can estimate the **dose and dosing interval** to maintain therapeutic levels.

Tabulations

Tabulations are pre-calculated **tables or charts** that provide dosing recommendations based on patient-specific or drug-specific parameters. These tables are often included in:

- **Drug handbooks**
- **Hospital dosing protocols**
- **Pharmacokinetic software and guidelines**

Common Tabulated Data Includes

Table Type	Purpose
Creatinine clearance vs. dose	Adjust doses in renal impairment (e.g., aminoglycosides, digoxin)
Weight-based dosing tables	For pediatric, obese, or underweight patients
Hepatic function tables	Adjust doses for drugs with hepatic metabolism
Toxicity thresholds	Guide dose reduction in toxicity-prone drugs (e.g., methotrexate)

Advantages of Tabulations

- Useful for drugs with complex or narrow therapeutic windows
- Reduces errors in drug dose calculation
- Helps guide dose adjustments based on lab parameters (e.g., renal/hepatic function)

Example: Gentamicin Dosing Table Based on CrCl

Creatinine Clearance (CrCl)	Recommended Interval
> 60 mL/min	Every 8 hours
40–60 mL/min	Every 12 hours
20–40 mL/min	Every 24 hours
< 20 mL/min	Every 48 hours or as needed

Nomograms vs Tabulations: Comparison

Aspect	Nomograms	Tabulations
Format	Graphical tools with scaled lines	Tables with pre-calculated values
Use	Estimate doses visually	Look up doses based on categories
Flexibility	Allows interpolation between values	May require rounding or adjustments
Speed	Very quick for experienced users	Slower but more intuitive for beginners
Accuracy	Depends on user accuracy in drawing lines	High accuracy (less prone to visual error)

Clinical Applications

- **Critical care dosing:** Rapid decisions for antibiotics like vancomycin or aminoglycosides
- **Therapeutic Drug Monitoring (TDM):** Especially useful for drugs with narrow therapeutic windows
- **Dose adjustment in renal failure:** Using creatinine clearance-based nomograms or tables
- **Pediatric dosing:** Weight or BSA-based tabulations are essential for safe prescribing

- **Chemotherapy regimens:** Dose based on body surface area (BSA) or liver functio

Limitations

- **Not suitable for all patients**: Unique pharmacokinetics (e.g., altered volume of distribution in sepsis) may require individualized dosing.
- **May oversimplify complex cases**
- **Assumes average pharmacokinetics**, which may not apply to extremes of age, weight, or comorbidities.
- **Dependent on accurate clinical data**: e.g., renal function estimation errors can lead to wrong doses.
    - **Nomograms and tabulations** are essential, practical tools for designing safe and effective dosage regimens.
    - They complement pharmacokinetic equations and enhance **clinical decision-making**, especially in settings requiring quick or approximate dosing estimations.
    - While they **simplify complex calculations**, they should always be used alongside **clinical judgment**, **patient monitoring**, and, when needed, **therapeutic drug monitoring**.

Conversion from Intravenous to Oral Dosing

- Conversion from intravenous (IV) to oral (PO) dosing refers to the clinical practice of switching a patient's medication route from intravenous administration to oral intake.
- This practice is commonly implemented once a patient is stable, able to tolerate oral medications, and no longer requires the advantages of IV therapy such as immediate drug action or precise control of blood concentrations.

- The process is often referred to as **IV-to-PO switch therapy** and plays a crucial role in optimizing patient care, improving comfort, reducing hospital stays, and minimizing healthcare costs.

Rationale for IV-to-Oral Conversion

- **Improved Patient Comfort and Convenience**
  - Oral dosing is less invasive and more comfortable.
  - Reduces the risk of complications related to IV catheters (e.g., phlebitis, infection).
- **Cost Effectiveness**
  - IV medications are generally more expensive due to the cost of formulation, administration equipment, and nursing time.
  - Oral therapy reduces hospitalization time and nursing care burden.
- **Decreased Risk of IV-related Complications**
  - Avoids complications like thrombophlebitis, catheter-related bloodstream infections, and fluid overload.
- **Facilitates Early Discharge**
  - Patients can be discharged earlier when switched to oral medication, especially in the context of antibiotic therapy.

Criteria for IV-to-Oral Conversion

- The decision to switch from IV to PO must be based on both clinical judgment and evidence-based protocols. The criteria generally include

1. Clinical Stability

- Normal or improving vital signs
- Afebrile for 24–48 hours
- Resolution or improvement of infection/inflammation signs

2. Functional Gastrointestinal (GI) Tract

- Patient is able to swallow and absorb oral medications
- No persistent nausea, vomiting, diarrhea, or GI bleeding
- No conditions requiring NPO (nothing by mouth) status

3. Available Oral Formulation

- Equivalent or therapeutically effective oral formulation is available
- Oral bioavailability is sufficient to achieve desired therapeutic levels

4. No Drug Interaction or Contraindications

- Oral medication is not contraindicated in the presence of other medications, food interactions, or disease states

Types of IV-to-PO Conversions

- There are three main types of conversions depending on the drug characteristics

1. Direct (Equivalent) Switch

- Drug has excellent oral bioavailability (usually ≥90%)
- Oral dose is equivalent to IV dose
- Example: Levofloxacin, Metronidazole, Fluconazole

2. Sequential Therapy

- Same compound but requires dose adjustment due to different bioavailability
- Example: Ciprofloxacin IV (400 mg) ≈ Ciprofloxacin PO (500–750 mg)

3. Therapeutic Substitution

- IV drug is substituted with an oral drug from the same class or with similar activity
- Used when no oral formulation of the same drug is available
- Example: IV Ampicillin → PO Amoxicillin

Steps in the Conversion Process

- **Assess Patient Eligibility**
  - ➢ Review patient's clinical status and GI function.
- **Review Medication Properties**
  - ➢ Consider oral bioavailability, half-life, and pharmacodynamics.
- **Select Oral Equivalent**
  - ➢ Use dosing guidelines or conversion charts to determine equivalent oral dose.
- **Monitor Response**
  - ➢ Observe for therapeutic effectiveness and potential side effects after the switch.
- **Document and Educate**
  - ➢ Document rationale and educate patient/caregivers about the new regimen.

Examples of Common IV-to-Oral Conversions

Medication (IV)	Oral Equivalent	Bioavailability (%)	Notes
Levofloxacin 500 mg IV	Levofloxacin 500 mg PO	~99%	Direct switch possible
Metronidazole 500 mg IV	Metronidazole 500 mg PO	~100%	Excellent PO absorption
Ciprofloxacin 400 mg IV	Ciprofloxacin 500–750 mg PO	~70%	Requires dose adjustment
Fluconazole 400 mg IV	Fluconazole 400 mg PO	~90–95%	Direct switch
Morphine IV	Oral morphine (adjust dose)	~30–40%	Adjust dose due to lower PO bioavailability

Barriers to IV-to-Oral Conversion

- Lack of clear institutional policies or protocols
- Physician hesitation due to perceived risk
- Poor communication among healthcare team
- Patient factors such as vomiting or inability to swallow
- Drug-specific concerns (e.g., poor oral bioavailability, narrow therapeutic index)

Institutional Protocols and Role of Pharmacists

- Many hospitals establish **IV-to-PO conversion protocols** as part of antimicrobial stewardship or cost-containment initiatives.
- Pharmacists often play a central role by:
  - Identifying eligible patients
  - Recommending appropriate oral alternatives
  - Educating prescribers and nursing staff
  - Monitoring therapy outcomes and adverse effects

- Conversion from IV to oral dosing is a clinically sound, evidence-based practice that promotes efficient and safe medication use in hospitalized patients.
- It contributes to reduced healthcare costs, minimized complications, and improved patient outcomes.
- A systematic approach—considering patient eligibility, drug characteristics, and proper monitoring—ensures the success of IV-to-PO conversion protocols.
- Institutions should support this transition through structured guidelines, interprofessional collaboration, and continuous education.

Determination of Dose and Dosing Intervals

- The **determination of dose and dosing intervals** is a fundamental aspect of pharmacotherapy.
- It involves selecting the correct amount of a drug (dose) and how often it should be administered (dosing interval) to achieve optimal therapeutic effects while minimizing adverse effects.
- These decisions are grounded in principles of **pharmacokinetics (PK)** and **pharmacodynamics (PD)** and must be individualized based on patient-specific factors, the nature of the disease, and the characteristics of the drug.

Dose

- The amount of drug administered at one time or per unit of body weight.
- Can be expressed as:
    - **Fixed dose** (e.g., 500 mg twice daily)
    - **Weight-based dose** (e.g., 5 mg/kg)
    - **Body surface area (BSA)-based dose** (e.g., mg/m^2) - used in chemotherapy

Dosing Interval

- The time between consecutive doses (e.g., every 6 hours, once daily).
- It determines how frequently the drug must be administered to maintain therapeutic levels.

Pharmacokinetic Parameters in Dose and Interval Determination

- Several PK parameters guide the determination of dose and dosing intervals

A. Half-life ($t^{1/2}$)

- Time taken for the plasma concentration of a drug to reduce by half.
- Determines how long a drug stays in the body and how frequently it needs to be given.
  - ➢ Short half-life → frequent dosing
  - ➢ Long half-life → less frequent dosing

B. Volume of Distribution (Vd)

- The theoretical volume in which the drug distributes throughout the body.
- Affects the **loading dose** needed to quickly achieve therapeutic levels.

C. Clearance (CL)

- The rate at which the drug is eliminated from the body.
- Helps determine the **maintenance dose** needed to keep plasma levels within the therapeutic range.

D. Bioavailability (F)

- The fraction of the administered dose that reaches systemic circulation.
- Important for oral vs. intravenous dosing.

Dose Calculation

A. Loading Dose (LD)

- Given to rapidly achieve therapeutic drug concentration, especially for drugs with a long half-life.

$$LD = \frac{C_{target} \times V_d}{F}$$

Where:

- Ctarget = Desired plasma concentration
- Vd = Volume of distribution
- F = Bioavailability

B. Maintenance Dose (MD)

- Maintains drug concentration within the therapeutic range over time.

$$MD = \frac{C_{target} \times CL \times \tau}{F}$$

Where:

- τ\tau = Dosing interval
- CL = Clearance

Pharmacodynamic Considerations

- **Minimum effective concentration (MEC)**: The lowest drug level at which therapeutic effect occurs.
- **Minimum toxic concentration (MTC)**: The drug level above which toxicity occurs.
- The goal is to keep plasma concentration **between MEC and MTC**.

Drug effect may be:

- **Concentration-dependent** (e.g., aminoglycosides): efficacy increases with higher peak concentrations
- **Time-dependent** (e.g., beta-lactams): efficacy depends on how long drug levels remain above the MIC (minimum inhibitory concentration)

Factors Influencing Dose and Dosing Intervals

A. Patient-Specific Factors

- **Age**: Neonates and elderly have altered metabolism and excretion.
- **Weight and BSA**: Affect drug distribution and elimination.
- **Renal and hepatic function**: Impair clearance; may require dose adjustment.
- **Genetic factors**: Influence drug metabolism (e.g., CYP polymorphisms).
- **Comorbid conditions**: Heart failure, liver disease, etc., affect PK/PD.

B. Drug Characteristics

- **Therapeutic index**: Narrow therapeutic index drugs require precise dosing (e.g., digoxin, warfarin).
- **Half-life**: Determines frequency.
- **Formulation**: Sustained-release vs. immediate-release.

C. Disease Characteristics

- **Severity and urgency**: Life-threatening infections may require high initial doses.
- **Site of action**: CNS, bone, or abscesses may require drugs with good tissue penetration.

Practical Examples

A. Antibiotics

- Aminoglycosides (e.g., gentamicin): Concentration-dependent killing → once-daily dosing
- Beta-lactams (e.g., penicillin): Time-dependent killing → frequent dosing or continuous infusion

B. Antiepileptics

- Phenytoin: Nonlinear kinetics → careful dose titration needed
- Loading dose often used to quickly achieve therapeutic levels

C. Anticoagulants

- Warfarin: Narrow therapeutic index → frequent monitoring of INR
- Requires individualized dose adjustment

Dosing in Special Populations

Pediatrics

- Immature liver/kidney function alters metabolism and clearance
- Dose often based on weight (mg/kg)

Geriatrics

- Reduced renal/hepatic function, altered protein binding
- Increased sensitivity to certain drugs

Renal Impairment

- Dose adjustments based on creatinine clearance (CrCl) or eGFR
- Use of dosing nomograms (e.g., for vancomycin)

Hepatic Impairment

- Adjust dosing for drugs metabolized in the liver
- Monitor for signs of toxicity

Monitoring and Dose Adjustment

- **Therapeutic Drug Monitoring (TDM)**: For drugs with narrow therapeutic index
    - Example: Digoxin, lithium, theophylline
- **Clinical response**: Adjust dose based on therapeutic outcome
- **Adverse effects**: Reduce dose if toxicity occurs

Drug Dosing in the Elderly, Paediatric, and Obese Patients

- Drug dosing is not one-size-fits-all.
- Different populations—especially the elderly, paediatric, and obese patients—have **unique physiological characteristics** that significantly impact drug **absorption, distribution, metabolism, and excretion** (ADME).
- Understanding these differences is critical to **optimize therapy**, **maximize efficacy**, and **minimize toxicity**.
- This is particularly important for drugs with narrow therapeutic windows or those that require precise therapeutic levels.

Drug Dosing in the Elderly

A. Physiological Changes with Aging

- Aging affects multiple pharmacokinetic and pharmacodynamic parameters

Parameter	Age-Related Change	Effect on Drug Dosing
GI absorption	Slightly reduced motility and blood flow	Generally minimal impact on absorption
Body composition	↑ Fat, ↓ total body water, ↓ lean mass	Alters volume of distribution (Vd)
Hepatic metabolism	↓ Liver mass and hepatic blood flow	Reduced metabolism of some drugs
Renal function	↓ GFR, renal blood flow, tubular function	Reduced clearance of renally excreted drugs
Protein binding	↓ Albumin in some elderly	May increase free drug concentration

B. Pharmacodynamic Changes

- Increased sensitivity to CNS-active drugs (e.g., benzodiazepines, opioids)
- Altered receptor response (e.g., increased risk of orthostatic hypotension)

C. Clinical Considerations

- Start low, go slow: Begin with lower doses and titrate gradually.
- Monitor renal function using **creatinine clearance (CrCl)** rather than serum creatinine alone (due to reduced muscle mass).
- Use tools like **Beers Criteria** to avoid inappropriate medications.
- Increased risk of **polypharmacy** and **drug-drug interactions**.

Drug Dosing in Paediatric Patients

A. Paediatric Considerations by Age

- Paediatric patients are not just "small adults."
- Their organ systems are still maturing, which significantly alters drug disposition.

Age Group	Description
Neonates	Birth to 28 days
Infants	1 month to 1 year
Children	1 year to 12 years
Adolescents	13 years to 18 years

B. Pharmacokinetic Differences

Parameter	Neonates/Infants vs. Adults	Implication
Absorption	Delayed gastric emptying, variable pH	Altered oral drug absorption
Body composition	↑ Total body water, ↓ fat	Affects distribution of water/fat-soluble drugs
Hepatic metabolism	Immature enzymes (CYP450) in neonates	Reduced clearance of hepatically metabolized drugs
Renal function	Low GFR, tubular function in neonates	Prolonged half-life for renally cleared drugs
Plasma proteins	↓ Albumin and α1-acid glycoprotein	Increased free drug concentrations

C. Dose Calculation Methods

- Most pediatric doses are **weight-based**:

$$\text{Dose} = \text{Drug dose (mg/kg)} \times \text{Weight (kg)}$$

- **Body Surface Area (BSA)** method is often used in chemotherapy or critical care

$$BSA(m^2) = \sqrt{\left(\frac{\text{height (cm)} \times \text{weight (kg)}}{3600}\right)}$$

D. Clinical Considerations

- Use **pediatric-specific formulations** (liquids, chewables).
- Monitor closely for **adverse effects** and **therapeutic response**.
- Adjust dose as the child grows; regular reassessment is essential.

Drug Dosing in Obese Patients

A. Obesity and Physiological Changes

- Obesity affects the **volume of distribution** and sometimes **clearance**, especially for lipophilic drugs.

Parameter	Change in Obesity	Implication
Body fat	↑ Adipose tissue	↑ Vd for lipophilic drugs (e.g., diazepam)
Lean body mass	Also increases but to a lesser extent	May affect hydrophilic drug distribution
Liver function	Fatty liver may alter metabolism	Possible increased or decreased metabolism
Renal function	Often increased GFR in early obesity	May increase clearance for some drugs

B. Weight Metrics Used in Dosing

Weight Type	Definition	Used for
Actual Body Weight (ABW)	Total body weight as measured	Used for many drugs
Ideal Body Weight (IBW)	Based on height and gender	Used for aminoglycosides, some anesthetics
Adjusted Body Weight	Used when ABW is much higher than IBW	

C. Drug Characteristics and Dosing Decisions

Drug Type	Dosing Weight to Use	Example Drugs
Lipophilic drugs	ABW or AdjBW (Vd increases)	Diazepam, propofol
Hydrophilic drugs	IBW or AdjBW (less distribution into fat)	Aminoglycosides, vancomycin
Narrow therapeutic index	Use TDM and clinical monitoring	Warfarin, phenytoin

D. Clinical Considerations

- Be cautious of **overdosing** lipophilic drugs due to increased fat mass.
- Be cautious of **underdosing** hydrophilic antibiotics if using IBW alone.
- Use **TDM** (therapeutic drug monitoring) where applicable.
- Consider comorbidities (diabetes, hypertension) that may further impact pharmacokinetics.

Summary Table

Group	Key Challenges	Dosing Approach
Elderly	↓ Clearance, ↑ sensitivity, polypharmacy	Start low, go slow; monitor renal function
Pediatrics	Immature organs, rapid growth	Weight or BSA-based dosing; frequent reassessment
Obese	Altered Vd and clearance	Use IBW/AdjBW based on drug properties

- Drug dosing in special populations such as the elderly, pediatric, and obese patients requires careful consideration of physiological differences that influence pharmacokinetics and pharmacodynamics.
- A **personalized approach** that includes appropriate calculations, close monitoring, and frequent reassessment is critical to ensure safe and effective pharmacotherapy in these vulnerable groups.
- Awareness of these differences helps healthcare providers prevent therapeutic failures and minimize the risk of adverse drug events.

3. Pharmacokinetic Drug Interactions

- Pharmacokinetic drug interactions occur when one drug affects the **absorption, distribution, metabolism, or excretion (ADME)** of another drug.
- These interactions can significantly alter the **plasma concentration** of a drug, leading to **increased toxicity** or **reduced therapeutic effect**.
- Pharmacokinetic interactions are a major concern in clinical practice, especially in patients taking **multiple medications** (polypharmacy), the elderly, or those with **chronic diseases**.
- Recognizing and managing these interactions is crucial for **safe and effective pharmacotherapy**.
- The Drug whose Activity is affected by such an Interaction is called as a **"Object drug".**
- The agent which precipitates such an interaction is referred to as the **"Precipitant drug**".

Types of Pharmacokinetic Interactions

- Pharmacokinetic interactions are classified based on the stage of ADME affected

A. Absorption Interactions

- These occur when the **bioavailability** of a drug is altered due to the presence of another drug in the gastrointestinal (GI) tract.

Mechanisms:

- **Alteration in gastric pH**
- **Chelation or complexation** with other drugs or ions
- **Changes in gastrointestinal motility**
- **Interaction with drug transporters** (e.g., P-glycoprotein)

Examples

Object Drug	Precipitant Drug	Interaction Mechanism	Effect
Ketoconazole	**Antacids / H2 blockers**	Increased gastric pH reduces ketoconazole solubility	↓ Absorption
Tetracycline	**Calcium / Iron supplements**	Chelation forms insoluble complexes	↓ Absorption of tetracycline
Digoxin	**Metoclopramide**	Increases gastric motility	↑ Rate of absorption
Fexofenadine	**Antacids (aluminum/magnesium)**	Interference with drug transporter	↓ Fexofenadine bioavailability

B. Distribution Interactions

- These involve changes in how a drug is distributed in the body, especially **binding to plasma proteins**.

Mechanisms:

- **Competition for protein binding sites** (mainly albumin)
- Changes in **tissue permeability or blood flow**
- Most displacement interactions are transient and clinically relevant only for drugs with a **narrow therapeutic index** and high protein binding.

Examples

Object Drug	Precipitant Drug	Mechanism	Effect
Warfarin	**Sulfonamides / NSAIDs**	Displacement from albumin	↑ Free warfarin → ↑ Bleeding risk
Phenytoin	**Valproic acid**	Displacement + metabolic inhibition	↑ Free phenytoin → CNS toxicity

C. Metabolism Interactions

- The **most common type** of pharmacokinetic interaction.
- One drug affects the **hepatic enzymes** responsible for the metabolism of another, especially the **cytochrome P450 (CYP450)** family.

Mechanisms

- **Enzyme induction**: Increases enzyme activity → faster metabolism → ↓ drug levels
- **Enzyme inhibition**: Decreases enzyme activity → slower metabolism → ↑ drug levels

CYP Enzymes and Their Involvement

Enzyme	Common Substrates	Common Inhibitors	Common Inducers
CYP3A4	Statins, Benzodiazepines, CCBs	Ketoconazole, Erythromycin	Rifampin, St. John's Wort
CYP2C9	Warfarin, NSAIDs	Fluconazole, Amiodarone	Rifampin
CYP2D6	Beta-blockers, Codeine, Antidepressants	Quinidine, Paroxetine	Rifampin

Examples

Drug Affected	Interacting Drug	Mechanism	Result
Simvastatin	**Erythromycin**	CYP3A4 inhibition	↑ Simvastatin → muscle toxicity
Warfarin	**Fluconazole**	CYP2C9 inhibition	↑ INR → ↑ bleeding risk
Oral contraceptive	**Rifampin**	CYP3A4 induction	↓ Hormone levels → contraceptive failure
Theophylline	**Ciprofloxacin**	CYP1A2 inhibition	↑ Theophylline → seizures, nausea

D. Excretion Interactions

- These occur when one drug affects the **renal or biliary excretion** of another.

Mechanisms:

- Inhibition of **active renal tubular secretion**
- Changes in **urine pH** affecting reabsorption
- **Competition for transport proteins** (e.g., OATs, P-glycoprotein)

Examples

Drug Affected	Interacting Drug	Mechanism	Result
Penicillin	**Probenecid**	Inhibits tubular secretion	↑ Penicillin levels → prolonged action
Methotrexate	**NSAIDs**	↓ Renal clearance	↑ Methotrexate → toxicity
Digoxin	**Verapamil**	P-gp inhibition in kidney and gut	↑ Digoxin → bradycardia, toxicity

Clinical Implications of Pharmacokinetic Interactions

A. Increased Risk of Toxicity

- E.g., **Warfarin + Fluconazole** → INR ↑ → Risk of haemorrhage
- E.g., **Digoxin + Verapamil** → Bradyarrhythmia

B. Reduced Therapeutic Efficacy

- E.g., **Oral contraceptives + Rifampin** → Risk of pregnancy
- E.g., **Antibiotics + Oral contraceptives** (debatable) → Possible failure

C. Importance of Therapeutic Drug Monitoring (TDM)

- Essential for drugs with **narrow therapeutic index**: warfarin, phenytoin, digoxin, lithium
- Adjust doses based on plasma levels and clinical response

Strategies to Avoid or Manage Drug Interactions

- **Review medication history thoroughly**, especially in polypharmacy cases
- **Use drug interaction checkers** (clinical software/databases)
- **Choose alternative drugs** when possible
- **Stagger administration times** (especially for chelation or pH-based interactions)
- **Adjust doses** based on enzyme induction or inhibition
- **Monitor plasma levels** for high-risk drugs
- **Educate patients** about food-drug and OTC-drug interactions (e.g., grapefruit juice, St. John's Wort)

Summary Table

Interaction Type	Example Drugs	Result
Absorption	Antacids + Ketoconazole	↓ Absorption of antifungal
Distribution	Warfarin + NSAIDs	↑ Free warfarin → ↑ Bleeding
Metabolism	Simvastatin + Erythromycin	↑ Statin → Risk of rhabdomyolysis
Excretion	Methotrexate + NSAIDs	↓ Clearance → Bone marrow suppression

- Pharmacokinetic drug interactions can have serious clinical consequences, ranging from therapeutic failure to life-threatening toxicity.
- Understanding the mechanisms behind these interactions—absorption, distribution, metabolism, and excretion—is essential for **rational prescribing** and **patient safety**.
- Regular monitoring, awareness of high-risk drugs, and individualized patient care are key to managing these interactions effectively.

Inhibition and Induction of Drug Metabolism

- Drug metabolism is primarily carried out by enzymes in the liver, especially those of the **cytochrome P450 (CYP450)** family.
- The metabolic process transforms drugs into more water-soluble compounds for easier excretion.
- However, the activity of these enzymes can be altered by other drugs, environmental factors, or certain foods.
- This leads to **enzyme inhibition** or **induction**, both of which significantly affect drug concentrations in the body.
- Understanding these phenomena is critical to avoid **toxicity** or **therapeutic failure**, particularly with drugs that have a **narrow therapeutic index**.

Enzyme Inhibition

- Enzyme inhibition occurs when a drug (or other substance) **reduces the activity** of a metabolic enzyme, leading to **slower metabolism** of substrate drugs.
- As a result, the drug remains in the system longer, often at higher concentrations, which can **increase the risk of toxicity**.

Types of Inhibition

- **Competitive inhibition**: Inhibitor competes with the substrate for binding to the enzyme's active site.
- **Non-competitive inhibition**: Inhibitor binds elsewhere, altering enzyme structure and function.
- **Mechanism-based (irreversible) inhibition**: Inhibitor permanently deactivates the enzyme.

Onset and Duration

- Usually **rapid** in onset (within hours to days).
- Reversible unless the inhibitor is mechanism-based.

Examples of Enzyme Inhibition

Enzyme	Inhibitor Drug	Substrate Drug (Affected Drug)	Clinical Effect
CYP3A4	**Ketoconazole, Erythromycin**	Simvastatin	↑ Statin levels → Myopathy, Rhabdomyolysis
CYP2C9	**Fluconazole, Amiodarone**	Warfarin	↑ INR → Risk of bleeding
CYP2D6	**Quinidine, Paroxetine**	Codeine	↓ Conversion to morphine → ↓ Pain relief
CYP1A2	**Ciprofloxacin, Fluvoxamine**	Theophylline	↑ Theophylline → Nausea, Seizures

Clinical Significance of Inhibition

- Potential **toxicity** if dosage is not adjusted.
- Especially critical in drugs with narrow therapeutic windows (e.g., warfarin, digoxin).
- May necessitate **dose reduction** or **more frequent monitoring**.

Enzyme Induction

- Enzyme induction occurs when a drug or substance **increases the expression or activity** of metabolic enzymes, typically through enhanced gene transcription.
- This leads to **faster metabolism** of substrate drugs, often resulting in **lower drug levels and reduced efficacy**.

Mechanisms

- Activation of nuclear receptors (e.g., **pregnane X receptor [PXR], aryl hydrocarbon receptor**) which upregulate enzyme gene transcription.

Onset and Duration

- Slower onset (typically **days to weeks**).
- May persist for **several days** after stopping the inducer.

Examples of Enzyme Induction

Enzyme	Inducer Drug	Substrate Drug (Affected Drug)	Clinical Effect
CYP3A4	**Rifampin, Carbamazepine, St. John's Wort**	Oral contraceptives	↓ Hormone levels → Contraceptive failure
CYP2C9	**Phenobarbital**	Warfarin	↓ INR → Risk of clotting
CYP1A2	**Smoking (polycyclic hydrocarbons)**	Theophylline	↓ Drug level → ↓ Efficacy
CYP2D6	(Less commonly induced)	-	-

Clinical Significance of Induction

- **Loss of therapeutic effect** (e.g., anticonvulsants, immunosuppressants, contraceptives).
- Important to **adjust dosage** or switch to alternative drugs.
- Can **activate prodrugs** more quickly (e.g., increased conversion of codeine to morphine in ultra-rapid metabolizers if enzymes are induced).

Summary: Comparison Table

Feature	Inhibition	Induction
Effect on enzymes	Decreases enzyme activity	Increases enzyme activity
Drug levels	↑ Increased	↓ Decreased
Onset	Rapid (hours–days)	Slow (days–weeks)
Clinical consequence	Risk of toxicity	Risk of therapeutic failure
Management	Dose reduction or drug substitution	Dose increase or drug substitution

Case Scenarios

Case 1: Inhibition

A 55-year-old woman on **simvastatin** is prescribed **clarithromycin** for pneumonia.

- **Issue**: Clarithromycin inhibits **CYP3A4**, the enzyme that metabolizes simvastatin.
- **Risk**: Increased simvastatin levels → muscle pain, risk of rhabdomyolysis.
- **Solution**: Hold simvastatin or choose a different antibiotic (e.g., azithromycin).

Case 2: Induction

A 30-year-old woman on **oral contraceptive pills** starts **rifampin** for latent tuberculosis.

- **Issue**: Rifampin induces **CYP3A4**, which increases metabolism of estrogen and progesterone.
- **Risk**: Contraceptive failure → unintended pregnancy.
- **Solution**: Use alternative or additional contraceptive methods.

Food and Herbal Interactions

Agent	Type	Effect
Grapefruit juice	Inhibitor	Inhibits CYP3A4 → ↑ drug levels (e.g., statins)
Cruciferous vegetables	Inducer	Induce CYP1A2 → ↓ levels of some antipsychotics
St. John's Wort	Inducer	Induces CYP3A4 → ↓ effectiveness of many drugs

- Enzyme inhibition and induction are key components of **pharmacokinetic drug interactions**.
- Awareness of these processes helps clinicians **predict, prevent, and manage** potentially harmful drug interactions.
- Special attention is needed when prescribing drugs metabolized by **CYP450 enzymes**, particularly in polypharmacy settings, and with drugs that have **narrow therapeutic margins**

Inhibition of Biliary Excretion

- **Biliary excretion** is a significant route of drug elimination, particularly for **large, polar, or conjugated compounds**.
- Drugs are secreted by hepatocytes into bile and eliminated via the feces.
- This process is mediated by **active transport systems**, especially various **ATP-binding cassette (ABC) transporters**.
- **Inhibition of biliary excretion** occurs when a drug or compound interferes with these transporters, leading to reduced elimination of the affected drug.
- This can result in **drug accumulation**, **toxicity**, or **altered therapeutic response**.

Mechanism of Biliary Excretion

Steps in Biliary Drug Elimination

- **Uptake into hepatocytes** via transporters (e.g., OATPs).
- **Metabolism** (e.g., glucuronidation, sulfation).
- **Excretion into bile canaliculi** via efflux transporters.

Key Transporters Involved

Transporter	Full Name	Function
BSEP (ABCB11)	Bile Salt Export Pump	Secretes bile acids
MRP2 (ABCC2)	Multidrug Resistance-Associated Protein 2	Secretes conjugated metabolites
P-gp (ABCB1)	P-glycoprotein	Secretes many lipophilic drugs
BCRP (ABCG2)	Breast Cancer Resistance Protein	Secretes xenobiotics and drugs

Inhibition of Biliary Excretion

- Inhibition of biliary excretion refers to the **blockade or downregulation** of transporter-mediated drug excretion into the bile, leading to **accumulation in hepatocytes or plasma**.

Consequences

- **Drug accumulation in the liver or blood**
- **Cholestasis (bile flow impairment)**
- **Drug-induced liver injury (DILI)**
- **Reduced therapeutic clearance**

Mechanisms of Inhibition

- **Direct Inhibition of Efflux Transporters:**
  - ➢ Some drugs directly **bind to and inhibit** transporters like MRP2 or P-gp, reducing biliary clearance.
- **Competitive Substrate Inhibition:**
  - ➢ Two drugs may **compete** for the same transporter, reducing the excretion of one or both.
- **Downregulation of Transporter Expression:**
  - ➢ Some agents may **reduce gene expression** of transporter proteins, often through nuclear receptor pathways.

Examples of Inhibition of Biliary Excretion

Drug A (Affected Drug)	Drug B (Inhibitor)	Transporter Affected	Clinical Effect
Methotrexate	**NSAIDs, Probenecid**	MRP2	↑ Methotrexate → Myelosuppression, Nephrotoxicity
Ezetimibe glucuronide	**Cyclosporine**	MRP2, P-gp	↑ Ezetimibe levels → Enhanced effects, toxicity
Digoxin	**Verapamil, Quinidine**	P-gp	↑ Digoxin → Cardiotoxicity
Rifampin	**Cyclosporine**	P-gp, MRP2	↓ Biliary excretion → Hepatotoxicity risk
Rosuvastatin	**Gemfibrozil**	BCRP	↑ Rosuvastatin → Myopathy

Clinical Implications

A. Drug Toxicity

- Reduced biliary excretion causes **drug accumulation**, especially in hepatocytes.
- Examples: Methotrexate toxicity, digoxin toxicity.

B. Cholestasis and Liver Injury

- Inhibition of **BSEP** (Bile Salt Export Pump) can lead to **intrahepatic cholestasis** and **drug-induced liver injury (DILI)**.
- Example: Troglitazone (withdrawn from market due to hepatotoxicity via BSEP inhibition).

C. Altered Pharmacokinetics

- Increased systemic exposure of drugs when biliary clearance is blocked.
- May require **dose adjustment** or **avoidance of interacting drug**.

Special Considerations

1. Enterohepatic Recycling:

- Some drugs undergo enterohepatic circulation (e.g., oral contraceptives, mycophenolate).
- Inhibiting biliary excretion may **reduce recycling**, affecting therapeutic levels.

2. Liver Disease:

- Conditions like **cholestasis** or **hepatitis** can mimic or enhance the effects of transporter inhibition.

3. Drug Development:

- Biliary excretion studies are a key part of preclinical and clinical pharmacokinetic assessments to predict **DILI risk**.

Monitoring and Management

- **Avoid co-administration** of known inhibitors with drugs cleared via bile.
- Use **therapeutic drug monitoring (TDM)** where available (e.g., methotrexate, digoxin).
- Monitor for signs of **hepatotoxicity** (e.g., ALT, AST, bilirubin).
- Consider **alternative routes of clearance** if inhibition is unavoidable.
- Inhibition of biliary excretion is a significant cause of altered drug pharmacokinetics, especially in drugs that are **hepatically cleared**.
- It can lead to **drug accumulation**, **toxicity**, and **liver injury**.
- Awareness of the drugs involved, especially those affecting **MRP2, P-gp, and BSEP**, is critical for **safe prescribing** and **effective therapeutic management**.

4. Therapeutic Drug Monitoring

- Therapeutic Drug Monitoring (TDM) refers to the clinical practice of measuring specific drug levels in a patient's blood at designated intervals to maintain a constant concentration of the medication in the bloodstream.
- The primary goal of TDM is to optimize individual dosage regimens to enhance efficacy and minimize toxicity, especially for drugs with narrow therapeutic windows.

Rationale for TDM

- Not all drugs require TDM. It is particularly beneficial for medications that
  - Have a narrow therapeutic index (NTI)
  - Show significant pharmacokinetic variability among individuals
  - Require prolonged treatment
  - Exhibit a poor correlation between dose and therapeutic response
  - Have potentially serious side effects
- Common examples of drugs requiring TDM include
  - **Antiepileptics**: phenytoin, carbamazepine, valproic acid
  - **Antibiotics**: vancomycin, aminoglycosides (gentamicin, tobramycin)
  - **Immunosuppressants**: cyclosporine, tacrolimus
  - **Cardiac drugs**: digoxin, procainamide
  - **Psychiatric drugs**: lithium, certain antidepressants

Pharmacokinetics and TDM

- Understanding pharmacokinetics (PK) is crucial to TDM. It includes:
    - **Absorption**: How the drug enters the bloodstream
    - **Distribution**: How the drug disperses into body tissues
    - **Metabolism**: How the body chemically modifies the drug (usually in the liver)
    - **Excretion**: How the drug is eliminated (mainly via the kidneys)
- Factors such as age, weight, renal and hepatic function, genetic polymorphisms, drug interactions, and disease states can significantly influence pharmacokinetics, necessitating the use of TDM to personalize therapy.

The Process of TDM

- **Selection of drug and patient**
    - A drug suitable for monitoring is chosen, and a patient with variable drug response or high risk of toxicity is identified.
- **Sample collection**
    - Blood samples are usually collected at "steady state" (when drug intake equals elimination), often just before the next dose (trough level). For some drugs, peak levels (after dosing) may also be required.
- **Laboratory analysis**
    - Techniques like immunoassays, high-performance liquid chromatography (HPLC), or mass spectrometry are used to measure drug concentrations.
- **Interpretation**
    - Results are interpreted alongside clinical information, such as the patient's condition, lab values, and potential drug interactions.

- **Dose adjustment**
    - Based on the drug levels and patient response, clinicians may adjust the dosage to reach therapeutic levels.

Clinical Applications of TDM

- **Preventing toxicity**: For drugs like digoxin or aminoglycosides, TDM prevents life-threatening toxicities.
- **Ensuring efficacy**: Helps in titrating doses for effective treatment, especially in infections (e.g., vancomycin in MRSA).
- **Monitoring compliance**: TDM can detect non-adherence to prescribed therapy.
- **Managing special populations**: Such as neonates, elderly, or patients with renal/hepatic impairment.

Challenges in TDM

- **Timing of sample collection** is critical; wrong timing can lead to misinterpretation.
- **Interindividual variability** in pharmacokinetics requires precise calculations.
- **Cost and availability** of tests can limit widespread use, especially in low-resource settings.
- **Drug interactions** and comorbidities can complicate interpretation.

Future Directions

- **Pharmacogenomics**: Integration with genetic testing can further personalize therapy.
- **Point-of-care TDM**: Development of portable, rapid testing tools.
- **Artificial Intelligence (AI)**: Using predictive algorithms to improve dosing accuracy.

- Therapeutic Drug Monitoring is a vital tool in modern clinical pharmacology.
- By optimizing drug therapy based on measured drug levels and individual patient characteristics, TDM improves treatment outcomes and minimizes adverse effects.
- It represents a bridge between pharmacokinetics and personalized medicine, particularly in complex, chronic, and high-risk therapies.

Individualization of Drug Dosage Regimen

- Individualization of drug dosage regimen refers to tailoring the dose, frequency, and duration of a medication to suit the specific needs and characteristics of an individual patient.
- The goal is to optimize therapeutic outcomes while minimizing the risk of adverse effects.
- Since patients differ significantly in how they absorb, metabolize, and respond to medications, a one-size-fits-all approach is often inadequate, especially for drugs with narrow therapeutic indices.
- This need for personalization arises due to interindividual **variability**, which can be influenced by several factors including **genetic makeup**, **age**, **body weight**, **disease states**, and **concurrent drug therapy**.

Factors Affecting Individualization of Dosage Regimen

1. Genetic Variability (Pharmacogenetics/Pharmacogenomics)

- Genetic differences can influence both **pharmacokinetics** (how the body processes a drug) and **pharmacodynamics** (how the drug affects the body).
- **Polymorphisms in drug-metabolizing enzymes**:
    - Cytochrome P450 (CYP) enzymes are key players in drug metabolism.

- For example, polymorphisms in **CYP2D6, CYP2C9**, and **CYP2C19** affect metabolism of antidepressants, warfarin, and proton pump inhibitors, respectively.
- Individuals can be poor, intermediate, extensive, or ultra-rapid metabolizers, impacting drug levels and efficacy.

- **Drug transporters**:
  - Variants in genes encoding **P-glycoprotein (ABCB1)** can affect drug absorption and distribution.
- **Drug targets**:
  - Variants in receptors or enzymes (e.g., **VKORC1** for warfarin) can change drug response.

Clinical Relevance

- Genetic testing can guide dose adjustments. For example:
  - **Warfarin** dosing is adjusted based on CYP2C9 and VKORC1 genotypes.
  - **Thiopurine drugs** (e.g., azathioprine) require TPMT testing to avoid myelotoxicity.

2. Age

- Age significantly influences drug pharmacokinetics and pharmacodynamics.

Neonates and infants:

- Immature liver enzymes → slower metabolism
- Underdeveloped renal function → slower excretion
- Higher body water content → affects volume of distribution for hydrophilic drugs

Elderly:

- Reduced renal and hepatic function
- Changes in body composition (e.g., increased fat, decreased lean mass)
- Polypharmacy increases risk of drug interactions

Clinical relevance:

- Start with lower doses in neonates and elderly ("Start low, go slow" principle).
- Drugs like aminoglycosides or digoxin require careful monitoring.

3. Body Weight and Body Composition

- Body size affects the **volume of distribution (Vd)** and **clearance** of drugs.
- **Weight-based dosing** is standard for many drugs (e.g., chemotherapy, antibiotics).
- **Obesity**:
  - Lipophilic drugs (e.g., diazepam) have a larger Vd → require higher loading doses.
  - Clearance may increase or decrease depending on the drug.
- **Underweight/malnourished patients**:
  - Lower protein levels may lead to increased free (active) drug concentrations for highly protein-bound drugs.

Clinical relevance:

- Use of **ideal body weight (IBW)**, **adjusted body weight (ABW)**, or **body surface area (BSA)** for precise dosing (e.g., aminoglycosides, anticancer drugs).

4. Disease States

- Pathological conditions can alter drug metabolism, distribution, and elimination.
- **Renal impairment**:
  - Affects elimination of renally excreted drugs (e.g., aminoglycosides, lithium)
  - Dosing should be adjusted based on creatinine clearance or eGFR.
- **Hepatic dysfunction**:
  - Reduces metabolism of hepatically cleared drugs (e.g., theophylline, propranolol)

- Hypoalbuminemia affects protein-bound drugs (e.g., phenytoin)

- **Cardiac failure**:
  - Decreased perfusion → reduced hepatic and renal clearance
- **Gastrointestinal diseases**:
  - May impair drug absorption (e.g., celiac disease)

Clinical relevance:

- Liver and kidney function tests are essential before and during treatment.
- Adjust doses or extend dosing intervals accordingly.

5. Drug Interactions

- Drug interactions can be **pharmacokinetic** (affecting ADME processes) or **pharmacodynamic** (affecting drug action at the site).
- **Enzyme induction** (e.g., rifampin, carbamazepine) → increased metabolism → reduced efficacy of co-administered drugs.
- **Enzyme inhibition** (e.g., erythromycin, ketoconazole) → decreased metabolism → toxicity.
- **Protein-binding displacement** → increased free drug levels (e.g., warfarin interactions).
- **Synergistic or antagonistic effects**:
  - Additive toxicity (e.g., nephrotoxicity from aminoglycosides + amphotericin B)
  - Therapeutic antagonism (e.g., NSAIDs reducing antihypertensive effect)

Clinical relevance:

- Thorough medication review is essential before prescribing.
- Adjust doses or change drugs as needed to avoid adverse interactions.

Methods of Dosage Individualization

- **Empirical adjustment**:
  - Based on clinical response and side effects.
- **Nomograms and dosage guidelines**:
  - Used in renal/hepatic impairment or based on body weight/surface area.
- **Therapeutic Drug Monitoring (TDM)**:
  - Measures plasma drug levels to adjust dose (see previous explanation).
- **Pharmacogenetic testing**:
  - For drugs like warfarin, clopidogrel, codeine, and some anticancer agents.
- **Clinical decision support systems (CDSS)**:
  - Use algorithms and databases to guide dosing decisions based on patient data.

- Individualizing a drug dosage regimen is a cornerstone of **precision medicine**.
- It ensures that patients receive the right dose, at the right time, with minimal risk.
- By taking into account genetic factors, age, weight, disease states, and potential drug interactions, healthcare providers can significantly enhance therapeutic outcomes and reduce adverse drug reactions.
- As diagnostic tools and pharmacogenomic data become more accessible, individualization of therapy will become more routine and precise in clinical practice.

Therapeutic Drug Monitoring (TDM): Indications and Protocol

Indications for TDM (When and Why TDM is Used)

- Therapeutic Drug Monitoring is not necessary for all medications.
- It is primarily indicated when precise control of drug concentration is required to ensure efficacy and avoid toxicity.

The following are key indications for performing TDM

1. Narrow Therapeutic Index (NTI) Drugs

- These are drugs where the difference between the minimum effective concentration (MEC) and the minimum toxic concentration (MTC) is small.
- Small changes in concentration can lead to subtherapeutic effects or toxicity.

Examples:

- Digoxin
- Lithium
- Warfarin
- Theophylline
- Phenytoin
- Cyclosporine

2. Drugs with High Interindividual Pharmacokinetic Variability

- Some drugs exhibit significant variation in absorption, distribution, metabolism, or elimination among individuals, making fixed doses unreliable.

Examples:

- Tacrolimus
- Carbamazepine
- Valproic acid

3. Poor Correlation Between Dose and Clinical Effect

- When a drug's effect does not consistently correlate with its dose due to variable metabolism or elimination, TDM helps in adjusting dosage based on measured drug levels rather than clinical effect alone.

4. Risk of Toxicity

- Drugs that have potentially serious or irreversible toxic effects require monitoring to maintain safe plasma levels.

Examples

- Aminoglycoside antibiotics (e.g., gentamicin, amikacin) – risk of nephrotoxicity and ototoxicity
- Vancomycin – nephrotoxicity
- Lithium – neurotoxicity

5. To Ensure Patient Compliance

- TDM can be used to detect non-adherence in patients who are not responding to therapy or in those on long-term treatment regimens.

6. In Special Populations

- In certain groups like neonates, elderly, pregnant women, or patients with liver or kidney dysfunction, drug pharmacokinetics can change dramatically.
- TDM allows dose adjustments in these cases.

7. To Guide Dose Adjustment During Drug Interactions

- When a patient is on multiple medications that may affect the metabolism or clearance of a monitored drug, TDM helps to manage interaction-related changes.

- **Example**:

  Phenytoin levels may increase if administered with valproic acid, requiring dose modification.

8. During Changes in Clinical Status

- Acute illness, organ dysfunction, or initiation of dialysis can alter drug handling, warranting TDM.

Protocol for TDM (Step-by-Step Process)

- TDM must be carefully planned and interpreted.
- It involves coordination between clinicians, pharmacists, nurses, and laboratory personnel.

Step 1: Selection of Drug and Patient

- Choose drugs for TDM based on clinical guidelines and patient-specific factors.
- Evaluate whether the drug meets criteria for monitoring (e.g., NTI, variable kinetics, risk of toxicity).

Step 2: Timing of Sample Collection

- **Steady-State Level**: Most TDM measurements are taken after the drug has reached steady-state concentration (usually after 4–5 half-lives).
- **Trough Levels**: Blood is generally drawn immediately before the next scheduled dose — this reflects the lowest concentration and is most useful.
- **Peak Levels**: For some drugs (e.g., aminoglycosides), peak levels are measured 30 minutes to 1 hour after dosing to assess risk of toxicity.
- **Loading Dose**: When a loading dose is used, early monitoring may be performed.
- The timing must be documented accurately; wrong timing can lead to misinterpretation.

Step 3: Blood Sample Collection and Handling

- Use appropriate blood collection tubes (usually serum or plasma).
- Avoid contamination or hemolysis.
- Ensure proper labeling (with patient details, time of last dose, dose amount, and time of sample collection).
- Transport to the laboratory under specified conditions.

Step 4: Laboratory Assay and Analysis

- Choose a validated, accurate assay method based on the drug (e.g., immunoassay, HPLC, LC-MS/MS).
- The result should be expressed in terms of concentration (e.g., µg/mL or ng/mL).

Step 5: Interpretation of Results

- Compare measured concentration with therapeutic range.
- Consider
    - Time since last dose
    - Patient's age, weight, renal/hepatic function
    - Concurrent medications
    - Adherence
    - Clinical status

Example

- A low phenytoin level in a compliant patient with low albumin might actually reflect a therapeutic free drug level due to reduced protein binding.

Step 6: Dose Adjustment

- Based on the interpreted result, adjust the dose or dosing interval.
- Re-monitor as needed, especially after dose changes or if the patient's clinical condition changes.

Step 7: Documentation and Communication

- Record the result, interpretation, and clinical decision in the patient's chart.
- Communicate findings and actions clearly to all members of the healthcare team.

- TDM is an essential clinical tool for optimizing drug therapy in patients, especially those on drugs with narrow therapeutic ranges or altered pharmacokinetics.
- Proper adherence to the protocol ensures accurate, meaningful results that improve patient safety and therapeutic outcomes.
- As medicine advances toward personalization, TDM will continue to play a critical role in individualized pharmacotherapy.

Pharmacokinetic/Pharmacodynamic (PK/PD) Correlation in Drug Therapy

- Pharmacokinetics (PK) and pharmacodynamics (PD) are two essential disciplines in clinical pharmacology that describe different aspects of how drugs work in the body:
- **Pharmacokinetics (PK)**: What the body does to the drug – involving absorption, distribution, metabolism, and excretion (ADME).
- **Pharmacodynamics (PD)**: What the drug does to the body – involving the drug's mechanism of action, effect on target tissues, and clinical outcomes.
- **PK/PD correlation** refers to the relationship between drug concentrations over time (PK) and the resulting therapeutic or toxic effects (PD).
- Understanding this correlation is critical in optimizing drug dosing, maximizing efficacy, minimizing toxicity, and developing new drugs.

Importance of PK/PD Correlation in Drug Therapy

- Helps in **designing optimal dosage regimens**
- Provides basis for **therapeutic drug monitoring (TDM)**
- Predicts **clinical outcomes and side effects**
- Guides **antimicrobial stewardship** (e.g., determining appropriate antibiotic dosing)
- Plays a major role in **personalized medicine**
- Aids in **new drug development** and regulatory approval

Pharmacokinetic Parameters

- Key PK parameters that influence drug concentration at the site of action
    - **Cmax**: Peak plasma concentration
    - **Tmax**: Time to reach peak concentration
    - **AUC (Area Under the Curve)**: Total drug exposure over time
    - **Half-life (t1/2)**: Time taken for plasma concentration to reduce by half
    - **Volume of distribution (Vd)**: Indicates drug distribution in body compartments
    - **Clearance (CL)**: Rate at which the drug is removed from the body

Pharmacodynamic Parameters

- PD parameters describe the drug's effects:
    - **Emax**: Maximum effect a drug can produce
    - **EC50**: Concentration required to produce 50% of Emax
    - **Minimum Inhibitory Concentration (MIC)**: For antimicrobials, the lowest concentration that inhibits visible growth of a pathogen
    - **Therapeutic Index (TI)**: Ratio of toxic dose to effective dose

Types of PK/PD Relationships

1. **Direct (Immediate) Relationship**
    - Drug effect is directly proportional to its plasma concentration.
    - Example: **Morphine** – as plasma levels rise, so does analgesia.
2. **Delayed Response**
    - A lag occurs between drug concentration and observed effect, often due to
        - Time taken for distribution to the site of action
        - Indirect drug mechanisms
        - Biological cascade activation
    - Example: **Warfarin** - anticoagulant effect lags due to clotting factor turnover.

3. **Cumulative Response**
    - Effect increases with cumulative exposure over time, even if plasma concentration stays constant.
    - Example: **Cisplatin** – toxicity is more related to cumulative dose.

Pharmacokinetic/Pharmacodynamic Models

Mathematical models are used to describe and predict drug effects

1. **Linear/Log-linear models**:
    - Assume a direct relationship between concentration and effect.
2. **Emax (Sigmoid) Model**:
    - Describes saturable drug response:

$$E = \frac{E_{max} \cdot C^n}{EC_{50}^n + C^n}$$

Where **n** = Hill coefficient (slope), **C** = drug concentration.

3. **Time-kill models** (for antimicrobials): Relate bacterial killing over time to drug concentration.

PK/PD Indices in Antimicrobial Therapy

PK/PD correlation is especially well-developed in **antibiotic dosing**, where three key indices guide therapy

1. **Cmax/MIC**: Peak concentration to MIC ratio
   - Example: **Aminoglycosides**
   - Aim: High peak concentrations (concentration-dependent killing)
2. **AUC/MIC**: Area under the concentration-time curve to MIC ratio
   - Example: **Vancomycin, fluoroquinolones**
   - Aim: Balance between exposure and effect
3. **T>MIC**: Time above MIC
   - Example: **β-lactams (penicillins, cephalosporins)**
   - Aim: Maintain drug level above MIC for a significant portion of dosing interval (time-dependent killing)

Applications of PK/PD Correlation

1. Dose Optimization

- Ensures that plasma levels are sufficient to produce the desired effect without reaching toxic levels.
- For example, **phenytoin** requires careful dosing due to saturable metabolism (non-linear kinetics).

2. Antimicrobial Therapy

- Helps determine whether to give a drug once daily (concentration-dependent) or multiple times per day (time-dependent).
- Reduces resistance development by maintaining effective drug concentrations.

3. Oncology

- Cytotoxic drugs have narrow therapeutic indices.
- Dosing schedules are based on maximizing tumor kill while allowing recovery of normal tissues (e.g., bone marrow).

4. Chronic Diseases

- In diseases like **epilepsy**, **hypertension**, and **depression**, maintaining drug levels within a therapeutic window is essential to control symptoms.

Challenges in PK/PD Correlation

- **Interpatient variability** in drug metabolism and response
- **Difficulty in measuring effect site concentrations** (e.g., brain levels)
- **Disease-induced changes** in PK (e.g., sepsis, organ failure)
- **Complexity of drug action mechanisms** (e.g., indirect effects, feedback loops)
- **Limited data in special populations** (pediatrics, geriatrics, pregnant women)

Future Directions

- **Population PK/PD modeling**: Uses data from multiple patients to predict optimal dosing strategies.
- **Pharmacogenomics integration**: Combines genetic profiles with PK/PD data to personalize therapy.
- **Machine learning and AI**: Enhance prediction of drug response and automate dosage adjustments.
- **Point-of-care TDM devices**: Real-time data collection and interpretation for rapid decision-making.

- Pharmacokinetic/pharmacodynamic (PK/PD) correlation forms the foundation of rational drug therapy.

- It connects drug concentration-time profiles with therapeutic outcomes, allowing clinicians to personalize treatment for maximum benefit and minimal harm.
- With advancements in modelling, genetic testing, and real-time monitoring, PK/PD-guided therapy is becoming a cornerstone of precision medicine.

Therapeutic Drug Monitoring (TDM) of Drugs Used in Cardiovascular Disease

- Cardiovascular diseases (CVDs) such as arrhythmias, heart failure, hypertension, and ischemic heart disease are among the leading causes of morbidity and mortality worldwide.
- The pharmacological management of these conditions involves drugs that often have narrow therapeutic indices, complex pharmacokinetics, and significant inter-individual variability.
- Therefore, **Therapeutic Drug Monitoring (TDM)** plays a vital role in optimizing therapy, enhancing efficacy, and minimizing adverse effects.

Why TDM is Important in Cardiovascular Drugs

- **Narrow therapeutic range**: Some cardiovascular drugs can easily become toxic or ineffective with small changes in blood concentration.
- **Variable pharmacokinetics**: Differences in age, liver and kidney function, and drug interactions can significantly alter drug metabolism and clearance.
- **Critical clinical outcomes**: Subtherapeutic levels may lead to life-threatening arrhythmias or thromboembolic events; toxic levels can result in hypotension, bleeding, or cardiac arrest.
- **Polypharmacy**: Cardiovascular patients often take multiple drugs, increasing the risk of interactions.

Cardiovascular Drugs Commonly Monitored by TDM

1. Digoxin

Indication: Congestive heart failure, atrial fibrillation

Therapeutic Range:

- For heart failure: 0.5–0.8 ng/mL
- For arrhythmias: 0.8–2.0 ng/mL

Toxic Effects:

- Nausea, vomiting
- Bradycardia
- Visual disturbances (e.g., yellow vision)
- Arrhythmias (e.g., ventricular tachycardia)

Monitoring Notes:

- Measure **trough level** 6–8 hours after last dose.
- Adjust dose in **renal impairment**.
- Interactions with **verapamil, amiodarone, quinidine**, and **loop diuretics** (due to hypokalemia).

2. Antiarrhythmic Drugs

a. Amiodarone

Indication: Ventricular and supraventricular arrhythmias

Therapeutic Range: 0.5–2.5 μg/mL

Toxic Effects:

- Thyroid dysfunction
- Pulmonary fibrosis
- Liver toxicity
- Corneal deposits

Monitoring Notes:

- Long half-life (20–100 days); TDM is not routine but may be helpful in long-term therapy or toxicity.
- Monitor liver, thyroid, and lung function regularly.

b. Procainamide

Indication: Ventricular arrhythmias

Therapeutic Range:

- Procainamide: 4–10 μg/mL
- N-acetyl procainamide (NAPA): 10–30 μg/mL
- Total (sum): 10–30 μg/mL

Toxic Effects:

- Lupus-like syndrome
- Agranulocytosis
- Cardiac toxicity (QT prolongation)

Monitoring Notes:

- Monitor both procainamide and its active metabolite (NAPA), especially in **renal dysfunction**.

c. Quinidine

Therapeutic Range: 2–6 μg/mL

Toxic Effects:

- Cinchonism (headache, tinnitus, dizziness)
- Arrhythmias (torsades de pointes)
- Gastrointestinal upset

3. Anticoagulants

a. Warfarin

Indication: Prevention and treatment of thromboembolism (DVT, PE, atrial fibrillation, prosthetic heart valves)

Therapeutic Monitoring Parameter:

- **INR (International Normalized Ratio)**
  - ➢ Target INR: 2.0–3.0 for most indications
  - ➢ Target INR: 2.5–3.5 for mechanical heart valves

Toxic Effects:

- ➢ Bleeding
- ➢ Skin necrosis
- ➢ Purple toe syndrome

Monitoring Notes:

- ➢ Not TDM in the traditional sense (not measuring blood levels of warfarin), but INR serves as a pharmacodynamic surrogate.
- ➢ Interactions with **vitamin K-containing foods**, antibiotics, NSAIDs, and numerous drugs.

b. Heparin (Unfractionated)

Monitoring Parameter: aPTT (activated partial thromboplastin time)

- Target: 1.5–2.5 times control

Low Molecular Weight Heparin (LMWH):

- **Anti-factor Xa levels** measured in special populations (e.g., renal impairment, obesity, pregnancy).

4. Calcium Channel Blockers (Rarely TDM)

- **Verapamil and diltiazem** may be considered for TDM in cases of suspected toxicity or drug interactions.
- Therapeutic ranges are not well defined for routine monitoring.

5. Beta-blockers (Limited Role in TDM)

- **Propranolol**: Sometimes monitored for performance anxiety or arrhythmias.
- Most beta-blockers do not require TDM due to wide therapeutic index.

General Protocol for TDM in Cardiovascular Drugs

Step 1: Patient Selection

- Those on NTI cardiovascular drugs
- Elderly or renally impaired patients
- Suspected toxicity or subtherapeutic response
- Potential drug interactions

Step 2: Sample Collection

- **Trough levels** generally preferred (immediately before the next dose)
- For **digoxin**, collect blood 6–8 hours post-dose to avoid falsely high results

Step 3: Laboratory Analysis

- Accurate assay methods (e.g., immunoassay, HPLC)
- Note factors that might interfere with assay (e.g., renal dysfunction, hypoalbuminemia)

Step 4: Interpretation

- Compare levels to standard **therapeutic range**
- Consider timing, dosage, patient factors, and clinical symptoms
- Adjust dose accordingly

Step 5: Re-monitoring

- After dose changes, monitor again after 4–5 half-lives or sooner in toxicity
- Regular monitoring for long-term therapy (e.g., digoxin, warfarin)

Challenges in TDM for Cardiovascular Drugs

- **Interindividual variability** in metabolism and response
- **Drug-drug and drug-food interactions** (especially for warfarin and digoxin)
- **Patient adherence**: Poor compliance can affect drug levels
- **Dynamic clinical conditions**: Changes in renal or liver function affect drug clearance and **need for specialized labs and trained personnel**

- TDM in cardiovascular pharmacotherapy is a critical tool for ensuring safe and effective treatment, particularly with drugs like **digoxin**, **warfarin**, **procainamide**, and **amiodarone**.
- By measuring drug levels or related pharmacodynamic parameters (like INR), clinicians can fine-tune therapy to the individual patient's needs.
- In an era of personalized medicine, integrating TDM with clinical judgment, genetic testing, and patient monitoring will continue to enhance cardiovascular care outcomes.

Therapeutic Drug Monitoring (TDM) of Drugs Used in Seizure Disorders

- Seizure disorders (epilepsies) are chronic neurological conditions characterized by recurrent, unprovoked seizures.
- **Antiepileptic drugs (AEDs)** are the cornerstone of therapy, aimed at achieving complete seizure control with minimal side effects.
- However, many AEDs have narrow therapeutic ranges, complex pharmacokinetics, and exhibit considerable interpatient variability.
- Hence, **Therapeutic Drug Monitoring (TDM)** is an invaluable tool in the management of seizure disorders.

Why TDM is Important in Seizure Disorders

- **Narrow therapeutic index**: Small differences in plasma drug levels can lead to toxicity or therapeutic failure.
- **Variable pharmacokinetics**: Factors like age, liver function, pregnancy, and drug interactions influence metabolism.
- **Non-adherence**: TDM helps assess compliance in patients with breakthrough seizures.

- **Chronic therapy**: Long-term AED use requires regular monitoring to avoid cumulative toxicity.
- **Polytherapy**: Many patients are on multiple AEDs, increasing the risk of pharmacokinetic interactions.

Goals of TDM in Seizure Disorders

- Optimize seizure control.
- Minimize adverse effects.
- Individualize dosing regimens.
- Assess adherence.
- Guide dose adjustments during physiological changes (e.g., growth in children, pregnancy).
- Identify potential toxicity or drug interactions.

Commonly Monitored Antiepileptic Drugs (AEDs)

1. Phenytoin

- **Therapeutic Range**: 10–20 μg/mL (total); 1–2 μg/mL (free)
- **Kinetics**: Non-linear (Michaelis-Menten); small dose changes can lead to large changes in blood levels
- **Toxicity**:
    - Nystagmus
    - Ataxia
    - Gingival hyperplasia
    - Hirsutism
    - Cognitive dysfunction

- **Monitoring Notes**:
  - Adjust for **hypoalbuminemia** or **renal failure** (free phenytoin may be more accurate)
  - Drug interactions (e.g., valproate, carbamazepine)

2. Valproic Acid (Valproate)

- **Therapeutic Range**: 50–100 µg/mL (may be up to 125 µg/mL in some cases)
- **Toxicity**:
  - Hepatotoxicity
  - Pancreatitis
  - Thrombocytopenia
  - Tremor
- **Monitoring Notes**:
  - Highly protein-bound; free level monitoring may be needed in low albumin states
  - Monitor **liver function** and **platelet count**
  - Interacts with **lamotrigine** (increases lamotrigine levels)

3. Carbamazepine

- **Therapeutic Range**: 4–12 µg/mL
- **Toxicity**:
  - Dizziness
  - Diplopia
  - Hyponatremia
  - Agranulocytosis
  - Hepatotoxicity

- **Monitoring Notes**:
  - Autoinduction: metabolism increases during the first few weeks, requiring dose adjustment
  - Monitor **liver function** and **CBC**
  - Induces hepatic enzymes → lowers levels of other AEDs

4. Phenobarbital

- **Therapeutic Range**: 15–40 μg/mL
- **Toxicity**:
  - Sedation
  - Cognitive impairment
  - Hyperactivity (in children)
- **Monitoring Notes**:
  - Long half-life (up to 100 hours); steady-state takes 2–3 weeks
  - Enzyme inducer – interacts with many other drugs

5. Ethosuximide

- **Therapeutic Range**: 40–100 μg/mL
- **Used for**: Absence seizures
- **Toxicity**:
  - GI upset
  - Lethargy
  - Blood dyscrasias (rare)
- **Monitoring Notes**:
  - Routine TDM not always necessary but useful in refractory cases or suspected toxicity

Newer Antiepileptic Drugs and TDM

- Newer AEDs (e.g., **lamotrigine**, **levetiracetam**, **oxcarbazepine**, **topiramate**) generally have wider therapeutic windows, more predictable pharmacokinetics, and fewer interactions, reducing the routine need for TDM.
- However, in specific situations, TDM may still be warranted:

Lamotrigine

- **Therapeutic Range**: 3–15 μg/mL (not universally established)
- **Toxicity**:
  - Rash (including Stevens-Johnson Syndrome)
  - Dizziness, ataxia
- **Monitoring Notes**:
  - Levels increased by valproate and decreased by enzyme inducers (e.g., carbamazepine)
  - TDM may help during **pregnancy** or **polytherapy**

Levetiracetam

- **Therapeutic Range**: 12–46 μg/mL (not well defined)
- **Toxicity**:
  - Behavioral changes
  - Somnolence
- **Monitoring Notes**:
  - Minimal metabolism, primarily renal excretion
  - TDM useful in **renal impairment** or for assessing adherence

Oxcarbazepine and Topiramate

- Routine TDM not usually required
- Consider monitoring in renal or hepatic dysfunction, or if toxicity is suspected

Protocol for TDM in Seizure Disorders

1. Patient Selection

- Patients with breakthrough seizures
- Suspected drug toxicity
- Non-compliance
- On polytherapy with interacting drugs
- Special populations (children, elderly, pregnancy, liver/renal dysfunction)

2. Timing of Sample Collection

- **Trough levels** preferred: collected just before the next dose
- **Steady-state** must be achieved (typically after 4–5 half-lives)
- For **phenytoin**, consider both total and free levels

3. Sample Handling

- Use serum or plasma depending on lab protocols
- Avoid hemolysis or improper timing, which may alter results

4. Interpretation

- Compare drug level to the **therapeutic range**
- Consider clinical symptoms, time since last dose, liver/renal function, protein binding, and drug interactions

5. Dose Adjustment

- Modify the dose based on the drug level, clinical efficacy, and side effects
- Use **pharmacokinetic formulas** in cases like phenytoin for precise adjustments

Challenges in TDM of AEDs

- **Individual variability**: Some patients may need levels outside the "therapeutic range"
- **Protein binding**: In low albumin states, total levels may be misleading
- **Non-linear kinetics**: Phenytoin requires careful titration
- **Compliance**: TDM can help, but interpretation must consider behavioral factors
- **Lack of clear therapeutic ranges**: For some newer AEDs, therapeutic ranges are not well established

➢ Therapeutic Drug Monitoring is a vital tool in managing seizure disorders, particularly with traditional antiepileptic drugs that have narrow therapeutic windows and complex pharmacokinetics.

➢ TDM aids in tailoring individualized therapy, especially during periods of physiological change, polypharmacy, or when treatment goals are not met.

➢ While newer AEDs may not routinely require monitoring, selective TDM can still offer valuable insights in complicated clinical situations.

➢ Ultimately, TDM should be used as a **complement to clinical judgment**, not a replacement.

Therapeutic Drug Monitoring (TDM) of Drugs Used in Psychiatric Conditions

- Psychiatric conditions, including **schizophrenia, bipolar disorder, depression, and anxiety**, are chronic and often require long-term pharmacological treatment.
- Many psychotropic medications—especially **antipsychotics, mood stabilizers, and some antidepressants**—have narrow therapeutic windows, significant inter-individual variability, and potential for serious side effects.
- In such cases, **Therapeutic Drug Monitoring (TDM)** plays a crucial role in optimizing drug therapy to enhance efficacy, minimize toxicity, and assess adherence.

Objectives of TDM in Psychiatry

- ➢ Ensure drug concentrations are within the **therapeutic range**
- ➢ Optimize **treatment response**
- ➢ Minimize **dose-related side effects**
- ➢ Assess **non-compliance** or **relapse**
- ➢ Guide **dose adjustments** in special populations (e.g., elderly, hepatic/renal dysfunction, pregnant patients)
- ➢ Detect **drug-drug interactions**

Psychiatric Drugs Commonly Monitored by TDM

1. Lithium

- **Used for**: Bipolar disorder (mania and maintenance)
- **Therapeutic Range**:
  - Acute mania: 0.8–1.2 mEq/L
  - Maintenance: 0.6–1.0 mEq/L
- **Toxicity**:
  - GI upset, tremor, confusion, ataxia, seizures
  - Renal dysfunction
  - Hypothyroidism
- **Monitoring Notes**:
  - Trough levels taken **12 hours after last dose**
  - Narrow therapeutic index—monitor frequently during dose initiation and titration
  - Adjust dose in **renal impairment**
  - Monitor **renal and thyroid function** periodically
  - Interactions: NSAIDs, ACE inhibitors, diuretics (especially thiazides) increase lithium levels

2. Tricyclic Antidepressants (TCAs)

Examples: Amitriptyline, Nortriptyline, Imipramine, Desipramine

- **Used for**: Major depressive disorder, neuropathic pain, anxiety
- **Therapeutic Range**:
  - Amitriptyline + Nortriptyline (active metabolite): 120–250 ng/mL
  - Nortriptyline: 50–150 ng/mL
  - Imipramine + Desipramine: 150–300 ng/mL

- **Toxicity**:
  - Anticholinergic effects: dry mouth, blurred vision, constipation
  - Cardiotoxicity: QT prolongation, arrhythmias
  - CNS effects: confusion, seizures (especially in overdose)
- **Monitoring Notes**:
  - Steady state reached in 4–5 days
  - Trough levels preferred
  - Genetic variability in CYP2D6 affects metabolism
  - Useful in **treatment-resistant depression** and **suspected toxicity**

3. Antipsychotics

a. Clozapine

- **Used for**: Treatment-resistant schizophrenia
- **Therapeutic Range**: 350–600 ng/mL
- **Toxicity**:
  - Agranulocytosis
  - Seizures
  - Myocarditis
  - Sedation, weight gain, metabolic syndrome
- **Monitoring Notes**:
  - Trough levels measured after achieving steady state (usually after 5 days)
  - Monitor **WBC count** and **ANC (absolute neutrophil count)** regularly
  - Smoking induces metabolism (CYP1A2)—may require dose adjustment if smoking status changes

b. Olanzapine, Risperidone, Haloperidol, Quetiapine

- **TDM Role**: Less established but may be useful in:
  - Poor clinical response
  - Side effects
  - Suspected non-adherence
- **Therapeutic Ranges** (approximate):
  - Risperidone + 9-hydroxy metabolite: 20–60 ng/mL
  - Haloperidol: 5–20 ng/mL
  - Olanzapine: 20–80 ng/mL
  - Quetiapine: 100–500 ng/mL

4. Selective Serotonin Reuptake Inhibitors (SSRIs)

Examples: Fluoxetine, Sertraline, Paroxetine, Citalopram

- **Used for**: Depression, anxiety, OCD, PTSD
- **TDM Role**:
  - Routine TDM not recommended due to wide therapeutic index
  - May be useful in:
    - Poor response
    - Adverse effects
    - Elderly or liver dysfunction
- Fluoxetine has a long half-life and active metabolite (norfluoxetine)
- Paroxetine: strong CYP2D6 inhibitor → drug interactions

5. Mood Stabilizers (Other than Lithium)

a. Valproic Acid

- **Used for**: Bipolar disorder (mania), epilepsy
- **Therapeutic Range**: 50–100 μg/mL

- **Toxicity**:
  - Hepatotoxicity, weight gain, tremor, pancreatitis
- **Monitoring Notes**:
  - Monitor liver function and platelets
  - Levels increase when co-administered with **lamotrigine**
  - Free levels may be needed in hypoalbuminemia

b. Carbamazepine

- **Used for**: Bipolar disorder (especially in rapid cyclers), epilepsy
- **Therapeutic Range**: 4–12 µg/mL
- **Monitoring Notes**:
  - Autoinduction occurs in the first 2–4 weeks
  - Monitor **CBC** and **LFTs**

6. Lamotrigine

- **Used for**: Bipolar depression, epilepsy
- **Therapeutic Range**: 3–15 µg/mL (not universally defined)
- **TDM Use**:
  - In pregnancy
  - With valproate (which increases lamotrigine levels)
  - For assessing compliance

General Protocol for TDM in Psychiatric Medications

1. Patient Selection

- Non-responders to standard doses
- Suspected drug toxicity
- Non-adherence
- Patients with hepatic or renal impairment
- Pregnant or elderly patients
- Polypharmacy

2. Timing of Blood Sample Collection

- **Trough level** (just before next dose) is usually ideal
- For lithium: sample 12 hours after last dose
- After reaching **steady state** (4–5 half-lives)

3. Sample Handling

- Serum or plasma, depending on the assay
- Avoid hemolysis
- Maintain accurate timing and documentation

4. Interpretation of Results

- Compare measured levels to therapeutic range
- Evaluate clinical response and side effects
- Consider patient-specific factors (age, renal function, albumin levels, drug interactions)

5. Adjustments and Follow-up

- Dose adjustments based on pharmacokinetic principles
- Re-monitor after 4–5 half-lives
- Regular follow-up in long-term therapy or when switching drugs

Challenges in TDM for Psychiatric Drugs

- **Interindividual variability**: Genetic differences in metabolism (e.g., CYP2D6 polymorphisms)
- **Wide therapeutic ranges** for some drugs (e.g., SSRIs) limit usefulness
- **Lack of standardized therapeutic ranges** for newer agents
- **Patient non-compliance**: TDM can detect but not always explain poor adherence
- **Clinical judgment required**: TDM is adjunctive, not a replacement for clinical evaluation

- Therapeutic Drug Monitoring is a valuable tool in psychiatric pharmacotherapy, especially for drugs with narrow therapeutic windows like **lithium, TCAs, clozapine, and valproate**.
- It helps optimize dosing, minimize adverse effects, and improve treatment outcomes.
- While routine TDM is not necessary for all psychiatric drugs, selective use in specific clinical scenarios—non-response, toxicity, pregnancy, or polypharmacy—can greatly enhance the safety and efficacy of psychiatric care.
- As psychiatry moves toward personalized medicine, TDM, combined with pharmacogenetics and clinical monitoring, will play an increasingly central role.

Therapeutic Drug Monitoring (TDM) of Drugs Used in Organ Transplantation

- Organ transplantation is a life-saving procedure for patients with end-stage organ failure.
- However, to prevent **allograft rejection**, transplant recipients must take **immunosuppressive drugs** for life.
- These drugs often have a **narrow therapeutic index**, **marked pharmacokinetic variability**, and potential for **serious adverse effects**.
- Therefore, **Therapeutic Drug Monitoring (TDM)** is crucial in the **management of immunosuppressive therapy** to maintain drug concentrations within a therapeutic window that minimizes rejection while preventing toxicity.

Objectives of TDM in Transplantation

- Prevent **acute and chronic rejection** of the transplanted organ.
- Avoid **drug-related toxicities** (e.g., nephrotoxicity, hepatotoxicity, neurotoxicity).
- Ensure **long-term graft survival**.
- Assess and promote **medication adherence**.
- Account for **pharmacokinetic variability** due to age, organ function, genetics, and drug interactions.

Key Immunosuppressive Drugs Monitored by TDM

1. Calcineurin Inhibitors (CNIs)

a. Cyclosporine

- **Mechanism**: Inhibits calcineurin, blocking T-cell activation.
- **Therapeutic Range**:
  - Varies by organ and time post-transplant.
  - **Early post-transplant**: 150–400 ng/mL (C0 or trough); **C2 monitoring** (2 hours post-dose) is more predictive of exposure (800–1500 ng/mL).
- **Toxicity**:
  - Nephrotoxicity
  - Hypertension
  - Hepatotoxicity
  - Hyperlipidemia
  - Gingival hyperplasia
- **Monitoring Notes**:
  - C2 levels correlate better with area under the curve (AUC) than trough (C0) levels.
  - CYP3A4 and P-glycoprotein substrate → susceptible to numerous **drug interactions** (e.g., with azoles, macrolides, rifampin).
  - Highly variable absorption → monitor closely during dose changes.

b. Tacrolimus

- **Mechanism**: Also inhibits calcineurin, more potent than cyclosporine.
- **Therapeutic Range**:
  - **Trough (C0)**: 5–15 ng/mL (varies with organ type and time since transplant).
  - **Liver transplant**: 5–10 ng/mL

- **Kidney/heart transplant**: 8–15 ng/mL (early), 5–10 ng/mL (maintenance)

- **Toxicity**:
  - Nephrotoxicity
  - Neurotoxicity (tremors, seizures)
  - Hyperglycemia
  - Hypertension
- **Monitoring Notes**:
  - Narrow therapeutic index
  - Metabolized by **CYP3A5** - genetic polymorphisms affect dose requirements.
  - Monitor closely during co-administration with inhibitors/inducers of CYP3A.

2. mTOR Inhibitors

a. Sirolimus (Rapamycin)

- **Mechanism**: Inhibits mTOR, blocking IL-2 mediated T-cell proliferation.
- **Therapeutic Range**:
  - 5–15 ng/mL (depends on combination with other immunosuppressants)
- **Toxicity**:
  - Hyperlipidemia
  - Thrombocytopenia
  - Impaired wound healing
  - Pneumonitis
- **Monitoring Notes**:
  - Long half-life (~60 hours) - steady state in 5–7 days
  - Monitor **trough levels** (C0)
  - Use whole blood (EDTA) for assay
  - Drug interactions similar to CNIs (CYP3A4 substrates)

b. Everolimus

- **Used in**: Kidney and heart transplants (as CNI-sparing therapy)
- **Therapeutic Range**:
  - 3–8 ng/mL
- **Toxicity and Monitoring**: Similar to sirolimus

3. Antimetabolites

a. Mycophenolate Mofetil (MMF) / Mycophenolic Acid (MPA)

- **Mechanism**: Inhibits inosine monophosphate dehydrogenase (IMPDH), blocking purine synthesis in lymphocytes.
- **TDM Use**:
  - Routine TDM **not recommended**, but helpful in:
    - Refractory rejection
    - Gastrointestinal side effects
    - Pregnancy
    - Pediatric or elderly patients
- **Target AUC** (12-hour): 30–60 mg·h/L
- **Toxicity**:
  - GI disturbances
  - Bone marrow suppression
- **Monitoring Notes**:
  - MPA undergoes **enterohepatic recirculation**
  - Protein binding variability → measure **free MPA** in hypoalbuminemia

b. Azathioprine

- **TDM Role**: Limited clinical use; replaced by MMF.
- **Metabolites** (6-TGN, 6-MMP) may be monitored in selected cases (e.g., non-responders, toxicity).

- **Toxicity**:
    - Bone marrow suppression
    - Hepatotoxicity
- **Genetic Note**: TPMT (thiopurine methyltransferase) activity affects metabolism - **genotyping/phenotyping** is useful.

4. Corticosteroids

- **Examples**: Prednisone, methylprednisolone
- **TDM**: Not routinely done due to:
    - Wide therapeutic window
    - High interindividual variability in effects
- **Clinical Monitoring** preferred (weight gain, hyperglycemia, infection risk)

TDM Protocol in Organ Transplantation

1. Patient Selection for TDM

- All transplant recipients on CNIs or mTOR inhibitors
- Patients with:
  - Rejection episodes
  - Toxicity signs
  - Drug-drug interactions
  - Hepatic/renal dysfunction
  - Pediatric/geriatric age groups
  - Pregnancy
  - Poor adherence

2. Timing of Sample Collection

- **Trough levels (C0)**: Collected **just before the next dose**
- For **cyclosporine**: Consider **C2** sampling for better correlation with efficacy
- Samples should be collected at **steady state** (typically 3–5 half-lives after dose change)

3. Sample Handling

- Use **whole blood (EDTA tubes)** for CNIs and mTOR inhibitors
- Maintain consistent timing and technique
- Avoid hemolysis and delays in processing

4. Interpretation and Dose Adjustment

- Compare measured level with target therapeutic range
- Consider:
  - Time post-transplant
  - Type of organ
  - Co-administered drugs
  - Hepatic and renal function
- Adjust dose cautiously, especially for drugs with **non-linear pharmacokinetics** (e.g., tacrolimus)

Factors Affecting Immunosuppressant Pharmacokinetics

- **Age**: Children often need higher doses/kg due to faster metabolism
- **Body weight and composition**
- **Hepatic and renal function**
- **Genetic polymorphisms** (e.g., CYP3A5 for tacrolimus, TPMT for azathioprine)

- **Drug-drug interactions**
    - **Enzyme inhibitors** (e.g., azoles, macrolides) ↑ levels
    - **Enzyme inducers** (e.g., rifampin, phenytoin) ↓ levels
- **Time post-transplant**: Immunosuppressant needs are higher immediately after transplantation

Benefits of TDM in Organ Transplantation

- Enhances graft survival
- Reduces incidence of rejection and infections
- Detects non-compliance
- Prevents drug-related toxicity
- Aids in optimizing dose in special populations

- Therapeutic Drug Monitoring is essential in organ transplantation to ensure the delicate balance between **immune suppression** and **drug toxicity**.
- Routine monitoring of **calcineurin inhibitors**, **mTOR inhibitors**, and selective monitoring of **antimetabolites** helps personalize therapy and improve outcomes.
- With the advent of pharmacogenetics and newer analytical methods, TDM is evolving toward a **precision medicine approach**, offering safer and more effective immunosuppression in transplant recipients.

5. Dosage Adjustment in Renal and Hepatic Disease

- Dosage adjustment in patients with renal and hepatic disease is critical due to altered drug pharmacokinetics (absorption, distribution, metabolism, and excretion) caused by organ dysfunction.
- In such patients, improper dosing can lead to subtherapeutic effects or toxicity.
- Below is a detailed discussion of the need, principles, and methods of dose adjustment in renal and hepatic diseases.
- Both the **kidneys** and the **liver** play essential roles in the elimination and metabolism of many drugs.
- In patients with **renal impairment** or **hepatic dysfunction**, drug clearance is often reduced, leading to prolonged half-life and drug accumulation.
- Understanding the pharmacokinetic changes and applying appropriate dose adjustments help prevent adverse effects while maintaining therapeutic efficacy.

Dosage Adjustment in Renal Disease

A. Renal Function and Drug Elimination

- The kidneys excrete many drugs and their metabolites via:
  - ➢ Glomerular filtration
  - ➢ Tubular secretion
  - ➢ Tubular reabsorption

B. Effect of Renal Impairment

- Renal impairment can lead to:
  - ➢ Decreased drug clearance

- Increased half-life
- Drug and metabolite accumulation
- Increased risk of toxicity

C. Assessment of Renal Function

1. **Serum Creatinine** - Often used but may be misleading due to muscle mass variations.
2. **Creatinine Clearance (CrCl)** - Estimated using:
   - **Cockcroft-Gault Equation:**

$$\text{CrCl (mL/min)} = \frac{(140 - \text{age}) \times \text{weight (kg)}}{72 \times \text{serum creatinine (mg/dL)}}$$

(Multiply by 0.85 for females)

3. **Estimated Glomerular Filtration Rate (eGFR)** - Calculated by MDRD or CKD-EPI equations; more accurate in chronic kidney disease.

D. Classification of Renal Impairment

Stage	GFR (mL/min/1.73 m^2)	Description
G1	≥90	Normal
G2	60–89	Mild
G3a	45–59	Mild-Mod
G3b	30–44	Moderate
G4	15–29	Severe
G5	<15	Kidney failure

E. Dosage Adjustment Strategies

- **Reduce Dose:** Lower the amount of drug per administration but maintain interval.
- **Extend Dosing Interval:** Keep dose same but administer less frequently.
- **Combination of Both**

F. Drugs Commonly Needing Renal Dose Adjustment

- Antibiotics: Aminoglycosides, vancomycin, penicillin
- Antidiabetics: Metformin, insulin
- Cardiovascular: Digoxin, ACE inhibitors
- Anticoagulants: Dabigatran, LMWH
- Analgesics: Morphine (active metabolites), NSAIDs

Dosage Adjustment in Hepatic Disease

A. Liver Function and Drug Metabolism

- The liver is responsible for:
  - Phase I metabolism (oxidation, reduction, hydrolysis) via cytochrome P450
  - Phase II metabolism (conjugation)

B. Effect of Hepatic Impairment

- Reduced metabolism → increased bioavailability (especially for drugs with high first-pass metabolism)
- Decreased plasma protein synthesis → increased free (active) drug
- Reduced bile excretion → accumulation of biliary-excreted drugs

C. Assessment of Hepatic Function

1. **Liver Function Tests (LFTs):**
   - AST, ALT, ALP, bilirubin
2. **Albumin and INR:** Reflect synthetic function

3. **Child-Pugh Score:**

- Parameters: Encephalopathy, ascites, bilirubin, albumin, PT/INR
- Class A (mild), B (moderate), C (severe)

Parameter	**1 point**	**2 points**	**3 points**
Encephalopathy	None	Mild	Severe
Ascites	None	Mild	Moderate
Bilirubin (mg/dL)	<2	2–3	>3
Albumin (g/dL)	>3.5	2.8–3.5	<2.8
INR	<1.7	1.7–2.3	>2.3

Total Score:

- 5–6: Class A (Mild)
- 7–9: Class B (Moderate)
- 10–15: Class C (Severe)

D. Dosage Adjustment Strategies

- **Avoid drugs with high first-pass metabolism** or reduce dose significantly.
- **Monitor free drug levels** for highly protein-bound drugs.
- **Avoid hepatotoxic drugs** or monitor closely.

E. Drugs Commonly Affected by Liver Disease

- Benzodiazepines
- Opioids (e.g., codeine, morphine)
- NSAIDs
- Statins
- Warfarin
- Theophylline
- Beta-blockers
- Calcium channel blockers

Practical Considerations

A. Drug Selection

- Prefer drugs with:
  - Non-hepatic/renal metabolism
  - Wide therapeutic index
  - Inactive metabolites

B. Therapeutic Drug Monitoring (TDM)

- Essential for drugs with narrow therapeutic ranges: e.g., digoxin, phenytoin, vancomycin

C. Clinical Monitoring

- Watch for adverse drug reactions and signs of toxicity
- Regularly assess renal/hepatic function

- Dosage adjustment in renal and hepatic disease is a complex but essential aspect of pharmacotherapy.
- Proper assessment of organ function and understanding pharmacokinetics of individual drugs are key to optimizing therapy.
- Clinicians must remain vigilant and apply evidence-based adjustments to ensure safety and efficacy.

Renal Impairment

- **Renal impairment** refers to a decline in kidney function that affects the kidneys' ability to filter waste products, regulate fluid and electrolyte balance, and perform other critical physiological functions.
- It may be acute or chronic and can progress to kidney failure if not managed appropriately.

Functions of the Kidney

- Filtration of blood to remove waste products (e.g., urea, creatinine)
- Regulation of fluid and electrolyte balance
- Acid-base homeostasis
- Regulation of blood pressure (via renin-angiotensin-aldosterone system)
- Production of erythropoietin (stimulates red blood cell production)
- Activation of vitamin D (for calcium metabolism)

Types of Renal Impairment

A. Acute Kidney Injury (AKI)

A sudden and often reversible decline in renal function over hours to days.

Causes:

1. **Pre-renal**: Hypovolemia, shock, heart failure
2. **Intrinsic (intra-renal)**: Acute tubular necrosis, glomerulonephritis
3. **Post-renal**: Obstruction (e.g., kidney stones, enlarged prostate)

B. Chronic Kidney Disease (CKD)

A slow, progressive, and usually irreversible decline in kidney function lasting more than **3 months**.

Common Causes:

- Diabetes mellitus (diabetic nephropathy)
- Hypertension
- Glomerulonephritis
- Polycystic kidney disease
- Chronic obstruction (e.g., stones, tumors)

Classification of Renal Impairment

Chronic Kidney Disease (CKD) Stages - Based on GFR (Glomerular Filtration Rate)

Stage	GFR (mL/min/1.73 m^2)	Description
G1	≥90	Normal or high with kidney damage
G2	60–89	Mild decrease
G3a	45–59	Mild to moderate decrease
G3b	30–44	Moderate to severe decrease
G4	15–29	Severe decrease
G5	<15	Kidney failure (end-stage renal disease)

Pathophysiology

In renal impairment

- **Glomerular filtration** decreases → accumulation of waste products (e.g., urea, creatinine).
- **Tubular reabsorption/secretion** is disrupted → electrolyte and fluid imbalances.
- **Hormonal functions** are impaired → anemia (due to decreased erythropoietin), bone disease (due to impaired vitamin D activation).
- **Acid-base balance** is affected → metabolic acidosis.

Clinical Features

A. Acute Kidney Injury

- Sudden oliguria or anuria
- Elevated serum creatinine and urea
- Fluid overload: edema, pulmonary congestion
- Electrolyte abnormalities: hyperkalemia, hyponatremia
- Nausea, vomiting, confusion

B. Chronic Kidney Disease

- Fatigue, weakness (due to anemia)
- Hypertension
- Edema (peripheral and pulmonary)
- Pruritus
- Bone pain, fractures (renal osteodystrophy)
- Uremic symptoms: nausea, anorexia, metallic taste
- Neuropathy in advanced stages

Diagnostic Evaluation

A. Laboratory Tests

- **Serum creatinine** and **Blood Urea Nitrogen (BUN)**
- **Estimated GFR (eGFR)**: calculated using formulas (e.g., MDRD, CKD-EPI)
- **Electrolytes**: potassium, sodium, calcium, phosphate
- **Urinalysis**: proteinuria, hematuria, specific gravity
- **Urine albumin-to-creatinine ratio (ACR)**

B. Imaging

- **Ultrasound**: to assess kidney size, obstruction, cysts
- **CT/MRI**: when structural abnormalities or masses are suspected

C. Biopsy

- Indicated in unexplained renal dysfunction, proteinuria, hematuria

Complications of Renal Impairment

- **Cardiovascular disease** (leading cause of death in CKD patients)
- **Anemia**
- **Bone and mineral disorders** (renal osteodystrophy)
- **Electrolyte imbalances** (especially hyperkalemia)
- **Metabolic acidosis**
- **Uremia** (toxicity due to retained waste products)

Management

A. General Principles

- Identify and treat the underlying cause
- Prevent further damage
- Manage complications
- Adjust medications (especially nephrotoxic drugs)

B. Acute Kidney Injury (AKI)

- Volume resuscitation (if hypovolemic)
- Remove nephrotoxic agents
- Correct electrolyte and acid-base imbalances
- Dialysis if necessary

C. Chronic Kidney Disease (CKD)

- **Blood pressure control**: ACE inhibitors or ARBs
- **Glycemic control** in diabetics
- **Dietary management**: low protein, low potassium/sodium

- **Erythropoietin** for anemia
- **Phosphate binders** and **vitamin D analogs** for bone disease
- **Dialysis** or **renal transplant** in end-stage renal disease

Drug Dosing in Renal Impairment

- **Reduced excretion** of drugs/metabolites leads to accumulation
- Use **Creatinine Clearance (CrCl)** or **eGFR** to guide dose adjustments
- **Monitor for toxicity**, especially for narrow therapeutic index drugs
- **Avoid nephrotoxic agents** (NSAIDs, aminoglycosides, contrast agents)

Prevention Strategies

- Control **diabetes and hypertension**
- Avoid **overuse of NSAIDs**
- Monitor **renal function** in high-risk patients
- Ensure **hydration** during contrast imaging
- Early referral to nephrologist

Dosage Adjustment in Renal and Hepatic Disease: Pharmacokinetic Considerations

- Drug dosing in patients with **renal** and **hepatic impairment** requires special attention due to altered pharmacokinetics (PK).
- The kidneys and liver are key organs for **drug metabolism and excretion**.
- Impaired function can lead to **drug accumulation**, **prolonged half-life**, and **toxicity**, or, in some cases, **subtherapeutic effects** if active metabolites are not generated.
-

- This necessitates **individualized dose adjustments** based on pharmacokinetic principles.

Basic Pharmacokinetics (ADME)

Pharmacokinetic Phase	Effect of Renal/Hepatic Impairment
Absorption	May be altered in uremia or portal hypertension
Distribution	Changes in protein binding (e.g., hypoalbuminemia) affect free drug levels
Metabolism	Hepatic dysfunction reduces Phase I/II enzyme activity
Excretion	Renal impairment reduces filtration/secretion of drugs/metabolites

Dosage Adjustment in Renal Disease

Pharmacokinetic Considerations

- **Reduced Renal Clearance:**
  - Drugs or metabolites excreted via the kidneys accumulate.
  - Common with water-soluble drugs (e.g., aminoglycosides, digoxin).
- **Altered Volume of Distribution (Vd):**
  - Fluid overload or protein binding changes may increase Vd.
  - Example: In uremia, acid-base imbalances alter protein binding.
- **Prolonged Half-life ($t^{1/2}$):**
  - Decreased clearance increases drug half-life → requires dose/interval modification.

Estimating Renal Function

1. **Serum Creatinine (Scr):** Alone is insufficient due to muscle mass influence.
2. **Creatinine Clearance (CrCl)** - Estimated using **Cockcroft-Gault Equation**:

$$\text{CrCl (mL/min)} = \frac{(140 - \text{age}) \times \text{weight (kg)}}{72 \times \text{Scr (mg/dL)}} \quad [\text{Multiply by } 0.85 \text{ for females}]$$

3. **Estimated GFR (eGFR)** - MDRD or CKD-EPI equation for CKD staging.

Dose Adjustment Strategies

Strategy	When to Use
Reduce Dose	To lower peak concentrations
Increase Dosing Interval	To avoid accumulation with unchanged peak
Combination of Both	For drugs with narrow therapeutic windows

Drug Classes Affected

Class	Examples	Adjustment
Antibiotics	Aminoglycosides, Vancomycin	Reduce dose and/or extend interval
Cardiovascular	Digoxin, ACE inhibitors	Monitor levels, reduce dose
Anticoagulants	LMWH, Dabigatran	Monitor coagulation, reduce dose
Antidiabetics	Insulin, Metformin	Adjust dose; metformin caution
Analgesics	Morphine (active metabolites)	Use alternatives like fentanyl

Dosage Adjustment in Hepatic Disease

A. Pharmacokinetic Considerations

- **Reduced Hepatic Metabolism:**
  - Impaired **Phase I (CYP450 oxidation)** and sometimes **Phase II (conjugation)** reactions.
  - Drugs with high hepatic extraction ratios are particularly affected.
- **Altered First-Pass Metabolism:**
  - Drugs with significant first-pass effect (e.g., propranolol) may have **increased bioavailability** in cirrhosis due to portosystemic shunting.
- **Reduced Plasma Protein Binding:**
  - Hypoalbuminemia → increased free (active) drug → higher risk of toxicity.
- **Impaired Biliary Excretion:**
  - Drugs excreted in bile (e.g., rifampin) may accumulate.

B. Assessment of Hepatic Function

- **Liver Function Tests (LFTs):**
  - ALT, AST, ALP, bilirubin
- **Synthetic Function Markers:**
  - **Albumin** (low in chronic liver disease)
  - **INR** (prolonged due to reduced clotting factor production)
- **Child-Pugh Score** - Commonly used to categorize liver dysfunction:

Parameter	1 point	2 points	3 points
Encephalopathy	None	Grade I–II	Grade III–IV
Ascites	None	Mild	Moderate-Severe
Bilirubin (mg/dL)	<2	2–3	>3
Albumin (g/dL)	>3.5	2.8–3.5	<2.8
INR	<1.7	1.7–2.3	>2.3

- **Class A** (5–6): Mild
- **Class B** (7–9): Moderate
- **Class C** (10–15): Severe

C. Dose Adjustment Guidelines

- **Child-Pugh Class A:** Usually no change, but monitor
- **Class B:** Dose reduction needed for hepatically metabolized drugs
- **Class C:** Avoid or significantly reduce dose of hepatically cleared drugs

D. Drugs Commonly Requiring Adjustment

Drug	Consideration
Benzodiazepines	Prolonged sedation due to slower clearance
Opioids	Accumulation of active metabolites (e.g., morphine-6-glucuronide)
NSAIDs	Increased risk of GI and renal toxicity
Anticoagulants	Warfarin: unpredictable INR, increased bleeding risk
Statins	Risk of hepatotoxicity; dose adjustment or avoidance
Beta-blockers	Increased bioavailability (propranolol)

Combined Renal and Hepatic Impairment

- In some patients, both renal and hepatic functions are impaired (e.g., hepatorenal syndrome).
- Drug dosing becomes highly individualized.
- Prefer drugs with:
  - Non-hepatic and non-renal clearance (e.g., metabolized by plasma enzymes)
  - Short half-life
  - Wide therapeutic index
- **Close monitoring** and **therapeutic drug monitoring (TDM)** is essential.

Therapeutic Drug Monitoring (TDM)

Indicated for drugs with:

- **Narrow therapeutic index** (e.g., digoxin, phenytoin)
- **Unpredictable pharmacokinetics**
- **Toxicity risks with accumulation**

Practical Approach to Dose Adjustment

- **Assess organ function**:
  - Renal: eGFR or CrCl
  - Hepatic: Child-Pugh score, albumin, INR
- **Determine pharmacokinetics** of the drug:
  - Route of elimination (renal vs hepatic)
  - Protein binding
  - Therapeutic index
- **Choose adjustment strategy**:
  - Reduce dose or increase dosing interval
  - Monitor drug levels and clinical response
- **Use available guidelines/tools**:
  - Renal dosing handbooks (e.g., Lexicomp, KDIGO)
  - Liver dosing references (e.g., FDA labels, clinical pharmacology resources)

General Approach for Dosage Adjustment in Renal Disease

- Renal disease significantly affects the excretion of drugs and their metabolites, especially those eliminated primarily by the kidneys.
- Impaired renal function can result in drug accumulation, prolonged half-life, and increased toxicity.
- Therefore, proper dosage adjustment is essential to maintain therapeutic efficacy while avoiding adverse effects.

Goals of Dose Adjustment

- Prevent drug toxicity due to accumulation.
- Maintain therapeutic drug concentrations.
- Ensure clinical efficacy.
- Reduce adverse drug reactions.
- Improve patient outcomes in those with chronic kidney disease (CKD) or acute kidney injury (AKI).

Factors Influencing Dosage Adjustment

- **Degree of renal impairment (GFR, CrCl)**
- **Drug characteristics:**
  - Route of elimination
  - Half-life
  - Therapeutic index
  - Active/inactive metabolites
  - Protein binding
- **Patient-specific factors:**
  - Age, weight, hydration status
  - Comorbidities (e.g., diabetes, heart failure)
  - Concurrent nephrotoxic medications

Step-by-Step General Approach

Step 1: Assess Renal Function

A. Estimation of GFR or Creatinine Clearance (CrCl)

- Serum Creatinine alone is not sufficient.
- Use formulas to estimate renal function:

i. Cockcroft-Gault Equation (most commonly used for drug dosing)

$$\text{CrCl (mL/min)} = \frac{(140 - \text{age}) \times \text{weight (kg)}}{72 \times \text{Scr (mg/dL)}} \quad (\times\ 0.85 \text{ for females})$$

ii. eGFR (MDRD or CKD-EPI)

- Used to stage CKD and in some clinical settings, but CrCl is preferred for many drug dosing guidelines.

Step 2: Review Drug Characteristics

Determine the pharmacokinetic profile of the drug:

- Primary route of elimination: Renal vs hepatic
- Fraction excreted unchanged in urine (fe): Drugs with fe > 0.5 typically need adjustment
- Volume of distribution (Vd) and protein binding
- Half-life ($t^{1/2}$): May be prolonged in renal dysfunction
- Active/toxic metabolites: Some are renally cleared (e.g., morphine-6-glucuronide)
- Therapeutic index: Narrow index drugs (e.g., digoxin, aminoglycosides) require close monitoring

Step 3: Determine if Adjustment is Necessary

Use reliable references:

- Drug databases (Lexicomp, Micromedex)
- Guidelines (e.g., KDIGO, FDA labels)

- Clinical Pharmacokinetics Texts

If the drug is not primarily eliminated by kidneys, dose adjustment may not be needed.

Step 4: Choose a Dosing Strategy

There are two main methods of dose adjustment:

A. Reduce the Dose

- Keeps dosing interval constant.
- Useful for maintaining steady-state concentrations with lower peaks.
- Appropriate for drugs with narrow therapeutic index.

B. Increase the Dosing Interval

- Maintains same dose size but increases time between doses.
- Useful for reducing drug accumulation while achieving therapeutic levels.

C. Combination Strategy

- Reduce both the dose and frequency.
- Used for drugs that are highly toxic or have long half-lives.

Step 5: Adjust the Dose Based on CrCl or eGFR

CrCl (mL/min)	Drug X Recommended Dose
> 60	100 mg every 8 hours
30–60	100 mg every 12 hours
10–30	100 mg every 24 hours
<10	50 mg every 24 hours or avoid use

Step 6: Monitor Patient Response

- Therapeutic drug monitoring (TDM) if applicable (e.g., vancomycin, phenytoin)
- Monitor clinical response and signs of toxicity
- Repeat renal function tests periodically, especially in unstable patients
- Adjust dosing again if renal function improves or deteriorates

Special Considerations

A. Dialysis Patients

- **Drug removal depends on:**
  - Dialyzer type (high-flux vs low-flux)
  - Duration and frequency of dialysis
  - Molecular size, protein binding, and Vd of the drug
- **Some drugs require post-dialysis supplemental doses (e.g., aminoglycosides).**

B. Nephrotoxic Drugs

Avoid or use with extreme caution in renal disease:

- NSAIDs
- Aminoglycosides
- Amphotericin B
- IV contrast agents

C. Narrow Therapeutic Index Drugs

Require more frequent monitoring:

- Digoxin
- Lithium
- Phenytoin
- Theophylline

Examples of Drugs Requiring Adjustment

Drug Class	Drugs	Considerations
Antibiotics	Aminoglycosides, Vancomycin	TDM essential; nephrotoxic
Cardiovascular	Digoxin, ACE inhibitors	Reduce dose; monitor K+ and renal function
Antidiabetics	Insulin, Metformin	Risk of hypoglycemia; metformin lactic acidosis
Anticoagulants	LMWH, DOACs	Adjust dose to avoid bleeding
Opioids	Morphine, Codeine	Active metabolites accumulate → use fentanyl
Anticonvulsants	Gabapentin, Pregabalin	Renally excreted → reduce dose

- Renal impairment significantly impacts drug elimination and necessitates thoughtful dose adjustment to prevent toxicity and ensure therapeutic efficacy.
- A systematic, patient-centered approach using clinical and pharmacokinetic principles ensures safe and effective drug therapy in patients with compromised kidney function.

Summary Checklist for Dosage Adjustment in Renal Disease

- Assess renal function (CrCl or eGFR)
- Review drug pharmacokinetics and renal excretion
- Determine if adjustment is needed
- Choose a dosing strategy (reduce dose, increase interval, or both)
- Refer to reliable dosing guidelines
- Monitor therapeutic response and renal function
- Re-adjust dose as needed

Measurement of Glomerular Filtration Rate (GFR) and Creatinine Clearance

- The **glomerular filtration rate (GFR)** and **creatinine clearance** are essential indicators of kidney function.
- They help assess how well the kidneys are filtering blood and eliminating waste products.
- Accurate measurement or estimation of these parameters is critical in diagnosing, monitoring, and managing kidney diseases.

1. Glomerular Filtration Rate (GFR)

- GFR is the volume of fluid filtered from the glomerular capillaries into the Bowman's capsule per unit time.
- It is typically expressed in milliliters per minute (mL/min).

Normal Values

- Normal GFR: ~90–120 mL/min/1.73 m^2 (adjusted for body surface area)
- A GFR below 60 mL/min/1.73 m^2 for three months or more is a marker of chronic kidney disease (CKD).

Methods of Measuring GFR

a. Direct Measurement (Gold Standard)

Involves using exogenous filtration markers that are freely filtered by the glomeruli and neither secreted, reabsorbed, nor metabolized.

Common substances used:

- **Inulin clearance:** Most accurate; rarely used clinically due to complexity and cost.
- **Iothalamate, iohexol, EDTA, or DTPA:** Radiolabeled or non-radioactive agents used in research or specialized clinical settings.

Procedure:

- Intravenous administration of the marker.
- Timed urine and blood samples are collected.
- Clearance is calculated using the formula:

$$\text{GFR} = \frac{U \times V}{P}$$

Where:

- UU = concentration of the marker in urine
- VV = urine flow rate (volume/time)
- PP = plasma concentration of the marker

b. Estimated GFR (eGFR)

- Widely used clinically, based on serum creatinine levels and patient characteristics.

Common formulas:

- Cockcroft-Gault equation
- Modification of Diet in Renal Disease (MDRD) formula
- CKD-EPI (Chronic Kidney Disease Epidemiology Collaboration) equation

CKD-EPI formula:

$$\text{eGFR} = 141 \times \min(SCr/\kappa, 1)^{\alpha} \times \max(SCr/\kappa, 1)^{-1.209} \times 0.993^{\text{Age}} \times [1.018 \text{ if female}] \times [1.159 \text{ if Black}]$$

Where:

- SCrSCr = serum creatinine
- κ\kappa = 0.7 for females, 0.9 for males
- α\alpha = -0.329 for females, -0.411 for males

Note: eGFR is an estimate and may be less accurate in extremes of body size, age, or muscle mass.

2. Creatinine Clearance (CrCl)

- Creatinine clearance is the volume of blood plasma that is cleared of creatinine per unit time.
- It approximates GFR, as creatinine is freely filtered by the glomerulus and only slightly secreted by the tubules.

Normal Values

- Males: ~95–140 mL/min and Females: ~85–125 mL/min

Measurement Methods

a. 24-Hour Urine Collection Method

- Involves simultaneous measurement of serum and urine creatinine.

Procedure:

- Collect all urine for 24 hours.
- Measure:
    - Total urine volume
    - Urine creatinine concentration
    - Serum creatinine concentration

Formula:

$$\text{Creatinine Clearance (CrCl)} = \frac{U_{Cr} \times V}{P_{Cr}}$$

Where:

- UCrU_{Cr} = urine creatinine (mg/dL)
- VV = volume of urine (mL/min)
- PCrP_{Cr} = plasma creatinine (mg/dL)

Adjusted for body surface area (BSA):

$$\mathrm{CrCl}_{\mathrm{adjusted}} = \mathrm{CrCl} \times \frac{1.73}{\mathrm{BSA}}$$

b. Estimation Using Formulas

Used when urine collection is impractical.

Cockcroft-Gault Equation:

$$\mathrm{CrCl} = \frac{(140 - \mathrm{Age}) \times \mathrm{Weight\ (kg)} \times [0.85 \text{ if female}]}{72 \times \mathrm{Serum\ Cr\ (mg/dL)}}$$

Comparison: GFR vs Creatinine Clearance

Feature	GFR	Creatinine Clearance
Substance Used	Inulin, iohexol, etc. (exogenous)	Creatinine (endogenous)
Accuracy	Gold standard	Approximation of GFR
Collection	Complex (blood + multiple samples)	24-hour urine + serum sample
Common Use	Research, specific clinical cases	Routine estimate in clinical practice
Tubular Secretion	No (ideal marker)	Slightly secreted → overestimates GFR

Clinical Importance

- **Diagnosis of CKD**: Persistent low GFR indicates kidney dysfunction.
- **Drug dosing**: Many drugs are renally excreted; dosing adjustments depend on GFR or CrCl.
- **Monitoring renal disease progression**.
- **Assessing kidney function before surgery or contrast imaging**.

Limitations

- **Creatinine clearance overestimates GFR** due to tubular secretion.
- **eGFR is unreliable** in:
    - Extremes of age or muscle mass (e.g., amputees, bodybuilders)
    - Acute kidney injury (serum creatinine lags behind actual function)
- **24-hour urine collection** is prone to errors (incomplete collection).

Recent Advances

- **Cystatin C-based GFR estimation**: A protein filtered by the kidneys, independent of muscle mass.
- **Iohexol clearance**: Emerging as a practical alternative to inulin for measured GFR.

Dosage Adjustment for Uremic Patients

- Uremia is a clinical condition resulting from severe kidney dysfunction, where the accumulation of waste products (such as urea and creatinine) leads to toxic effects in the body.
- In uremic patients, especially those with **chronic kidney disease (CKD)** or **acute kidney injury (AKI)**, the kidneys' ability to eliminate drugs and their metabolites is significantly impaired.
- Therefore, **dosage adjustment** of many medications is essential to avoid **toxicity** while maintaining **therapeutic efficacy**.

Why Dosage Adjustment Is Necessary in Uremia

- **Reduced drug clearance**: Decreased glomerular filtration rate (GFR) leads to slower elimination of renally-excreted drugs.
- **Accumulation of active or toxic metabolites**.

- **Altered pharmacokinetics**: Changes in drug absorption, distribution, metabolism, and excretion.
- **Changes in protein binding**: Uremic toxins can displace drugs from plasma proteins, increasing free drug levels.
- **Dialysis effects**: Some drugs are removed during dialysis, requiring post-dialysis supplementation.

Steps in Dosage Adjustment

Step 1: Assess Renal Function

- Use **eGFR** or **Creatinine Clearance (CrCl)** to quantify kidney function.
    - eGFR (CKD-EPI or MDRD formula)
    - CrCl (Cockcroft-Gault formula)

Step 2: Review Drug Properties

Key pharmacokinetic properties to consider

- Route of elimination (renal vs. hepatic)
- Therapeutic index (narrow vs. wide)
- Active metabolites and their elimination
- Protein binding
- Volume of distribution

Step 3: Choose Dosage Adjustment Method

Two main approaches:

- **Reduce dose** while maintaining the dosing interval.
- **Extend dosing interval** while keeping the same dose.

Sometimes a **combination of both** is required.

Step 4: Monitor Clinical Response and Drug Levels

- Adjust based on **therapeutic drug monitoring (TDM)** when available (e.g., for aminoglycosides, digoxin, vancomycin).
- Monitor for signs of toxicity or subtherapeutic effects.

Drugs Commonly Requiring Adjustment in Uremia

Drug Class	Examples	Notes
Antibiotics	Aminoglycosides, vancomycin, penicillins, cephalosporins, fluoroquinolones	Nephrotoxic potential, TDM important
Antivirals	Acyclovir, ganciclovir	Adjust to prevent CNS toxicity
Cardiac Drugs	Digoxin	Narrow therapeutic index
Anticonvulsants	Gabapentin, pregabalin, levetiracetam	Renally cleared, monitor levels
Antidiabetics	Metformin, insulin	Risk of lactic acidosis with metformin
Analgesics	Morphine, meperidine, NSAIDs	Avoid or adjust due to toxic metabolites
Anticoagulants	LMWH (e.g., enoxaparin), dabigatran	Adjust or avoid depending on drug
Psychiatric Meds	Lithium	Extremely narrow therapeutic index
Chemotherapy	Methotrexate, cisplatin	High toxicity potential

Drug Dosing in Dialysis Patients

Hemodialysis (HD)

- Drugs with **low molecular weight, low protein binding, and small volume of distribution** are likely removed.
- Administer certain drugs **after dialysis** (e.g., antibiotics).

Peritoneal Dialysis (PD)

- Less efficient than HD; slower drug removal.
- Dose adjustments differ and require individualization.

Examples of Dosage Adjustment

Aminoglycosides (e.g., Gentamicin)

- Renally cleared
- Dosage interval increased in renal impairment
- TDM used to maintain peak/trough levels

Digoxin

- Reduce dose and monitor serum levels
- Toxicity risk increases in uremia

Metformin

- Contraindicated if eGFR < 30 mL/min
- Risk of lactic acidosis

Vancomycin

- Adjust dose and interval based on CrCl and trough levels
- Avoid underdosing to prevent resistance

Dosage Adjustment Formulas

Adjusted Dose Formula

$$\text{Adjusted Dose} = \text{Normal Dose} \times \frac{\text{Patient's CrCl}}{100}$$

Or

use drug-specific adjustment tables provided in clinical resources or formularies like:

- **Lexicomp**
- **Micromedex**
- **AHFS Drug Information**
- **Renal Drug Handbook**

Monitoring and Precautions

- **Monitor kidney function regularly**, especially in patients on nephrotoxic drugs.
- Be cautious with drugs that have **narrow therapeutic windows**.
- Watch for signs of **drug toxicity** (e.g., confusion with digoxin, seizures with imipenem).
- Use **clinical judgment** along with lab values and patient response.

- ➢ Dosage adjustment in uremic patients is a critical aspect of safe and effective pharmacotherapy.
- ➢ Understanding renal function, the pharmacokinetic properties of medications, and individual patient factors allows clinicians to tailor drug regimens appropriately.
- ➢ Regular monitoring and consultation with pharmacists or nephrologists are essential to minimize risks and optimize outcomes.

Extracorporeal Removal of Drugs

- **Extracorporeal removal of drugs** refers to the elimination of drugs from the body using external methods that bypass normal physiological excretion, particularly in patients with impaired kidney function or drug toxicity.
- These techniques are commonly employed in **renal failure**, **drug overdose**, or **life-threatening toxicities**, especially when the body's natural elimination mechanisms are inadequate or compromised.
- Under normal conditions, drugs are primarily eliminated via hepatic metabolism or renal excretion.
- However, in certain conditions such as **uremia**, **acute kidney injury (AKI)**, or **intentional/unintentional overdose**, some drugs accumulate to toxic levels, requiring external means for removal.
- Extracorporeal techniques are particularly useful when the drug
  - Has a **low volume of distribution**
  - Is **poorly metabolized**
  - Is **water-soluble**
  - Has **low protein binding**

Techniques of Extracorporeal Drug Removal

A. Haemodialysis (HD)

Definition: A process where blood is filtered through a semipermeable membrane to remove waste products and drugs.

Mechanism: Diffusion of drug molecules across the dialysis membrane into a dialysate solution.

Drug Characteristics Favouring Removal

- Low molecular weight (<500 Da)
- Low protein binding (<80%)
- Small volume of distribution (<1 L/kg)
- High water solubility

Examples of drugs removed by HD

- Lithium
- Methanol
- Salicylates
- Ethylene glycol
- Theophylline
- Barbiturates

Limitations

- Not effective for highly protein-bound drugs (e.g., warfarin)
- Drugs with large volume of distribution (e.g., amiodarone) are poorly removed

B. Hemoperfusion

Definition: Blood is passed through a column containing adsorbent material (usually activated charcoal or resins), which binds and removes toxins and drugs.

Mechanism: Adsorption (not diffusion) is the primary mechanism.

Drug Characteristics Favouring Removal

- Highly protein-bound drugs
- Lipophilic drugs

Examples of drugs removed by hemoperfusion

- Theophylline
- Carbamazepine
- Phenobarbital
- Amitriptyline

- Phenytoin

Advantages

- Can remove protein-bound and lipophilic drugs
- Rapid onset of action

Disadvantages

- Risk of thrombocytopenia and hypocalcaemia
- Expensive and less widely available

C. Continuous Renal Replacement Therapy (CRRT)

Definition: A continuous dialysis technique used mainly in critically ill patients with unstable hemodynamics.

Types

- CVVH (Continuous Venovenous Hemofiltration)
- CVVHD (Hemodialysis)
- CVVHDF (Hemodiafiltration)

Advantages

- Gentle, continuous removal
- Better tolerated in hypotensive or ICU patients

Limitations

- Slower clearance compared to intermittent hemodialysis
- Less effective for drugs requiring rapid removal

Used for

- Vancomycin
- Beta-lactam antibiotics
- Some antiepileptics

D. Plasmapheresis (Plasma Exchange)

Definition: Removal and replacement of plasma to eliminate protein-bound toxins or antibodies.

Mechanism: Physical removal of plasma containing drug-bound proteins.

Effective for:

- Drugs with high protein binding and large volume of distribution
- Examples: Phenytoin, valproic acid, immune complexes, monoclonal antibodies

Limitations:

- Not effective for water-soluble, low molecular weight drugs
- Invasive and expensive

E. Peritoneal Dialysis (PD)

Definition: Dialysis performed via the peritoneal membrane in the abdomen.

Less efficient than HD, but used when:

- Hemodialysis is unavailable
- Pediatric or hemodynamically unstable patients

Drugs removed slowly, useful for:

- Lithium (mild toxicity)
- Methanol (if HD unavailable)

Drug Properties Affecting Extracorporeal Removal

Parameter	Favourable for Removal	Unfavourable for Removal
Molecular Weight	Low (<500 Da)	High (>1000 Da)
Protein Binding	Low (<80%)	High (>90%)
Volume of Distribution	Low (<1 L/kg)	High (>2 L/kg)
Water Solubility	High	Low
Endogenous Clearance	Low	High

Clinical Indications for Extracorporeal Drug Removal

- Severe poisoning or overdose
- Drugs with narrow therapeutic index
- Organ dysfunction (renal or hepatic failure)
- Failure of supportive care
- Presence of life-threatening symptoms (e.g., seizures, arrhythmias, coma)

Examples of Drugs Commonly Removed Extracorporeally

Drug	Preferred Technique	Reason
Lithium	Hemodialysis	Low protein binding, small Vd
Theophylline	Hemoperfusion or HD	Narrow TI, life-threatening tox
Methanol	Hemodialysis	Toxic metabolite, dialyzable
Phenobarbital	HD or Hemoperfusion	Long half-life, dialyzable
Carbamazepine	Hemoperfusion	Protein bound, toxic in overdose
Salicylates	Hemodialysis	Severe acidosis, dialyzable
Valproic Acid	Plasmapheresis or HD	High protein binding
Metformin	Hemodialysis	Lactic acidosis, water-soluble

Summary

Technique	Best For	Limitations
Hemodialysis	Small, water-soluble drugs	Not effective for lipophilic/protein-bound drugs
Hemoperfusion	Lipophilic, protein-bound drugs	Less available, costly
CRRT	ICU patients with unstable vitals	Slower drug clearance
Plasmapheresis	Drugs with high protein binding	Complex and expensive
Peritoneal Dialysis	Children, slow clearance needed	Inefficient, slow

- Extracorporeal removal techniques are vital tools in the management of drug overdoses and toxicity, especially in the setting of impaired renal function or life-threatening poisoning.
- The choice of method depends on the pharmacokinetic properties of the drug, the patient's clinical condition, and the availability of resources.
- Clinicians must consider drug-specific and patient-specific factors to decide on the most appropriate extracorporeal therapy.

Effect of Hepatic Disease on Pharmacokinetics

- The **liver** is a central organ in drug metabolism and elimination.
- Hepatic diseases such as **cirrhosis**, **hepatitis**, **fibrosis**, and **liver failure** can significantly alter the pharmacokinetics (PK) of many drugs, leading to changes in their absorption, distribution, metabolism, and excretion (ADME).
- Understanding these changes is critical for ensuring safe and effective pharmacotherapy in patients with liver dysfunction.

Overview of Pharmacokinetics (ADME)

- Pharmacokinetics describes how the body handles a drug through the following processes:
    - **Absorption**: Entry of the drug into the bloodstream
    - **Distribution**: Dispersion of the drug throughout body fluids and tissues
    - **Metabolism (Biotransformation)**: Chemical modification, primarily in the liver
    - **Excretion**: Removal of the drug from the body, primarily via the kidneys or bile

Hepatic Function and Drug Metabolism

The liver is responsible for

- **Phase I reactions**: Oxidation, reduction, hydrolysis (mainly via **cytochrome P450** enzymes)
- **Phase II reactions**: Conjugation (e.g., glucuronidation, sulfation)
- Liver disease alters these functions, affecting the metabolism and clearance of many drugs, especially those with **high hepatic extraction ratios**.

Types of Hepatic Disease Affecting Pharmacokinetics

- Acute hepatitis
- Chronic hepatitis
- Cirrhosis
- Fatty liver disease (NAFLD/NASH)
- Liver cancer
- Cholestasis or biliary obstruction
- Liver failure (acute or chronic)

Effects of Hepatic Disease on Each Pharmacokinetic Phase

A. Absorption

- **Portal hypertension** and **gastrointestinal edema** may impair drug absorption.
- **Reduced bile production** in cholestasis may affect the absorption of **lipophilic drugs** (e.g., fat-soluble vitamins, cyclosporine).
- **Delayed gastric emptying** is common in advanced liver disease, influencing drug onset.

B. Distribution

- **Hypoalbuminemia** (low albumin levels in liver disease):
  - Affects **protein binding** of highly bound drugs (e.g., phenytoin, warfarin, diazepam).
  - Leads to **increased free (active) drug** levels, raising the risk of toxicity.
- **Ascites and edema**:
  - Increase the **volume of distribution (Vd)** for hydrophilic drugs (e.g., aminoglycosides), leading to reduced plasma concentrations.

C. Metabolism – Most critical impact in hepatic disease.

Phase I Reactions (Cytochrome P450-mediated)

- Significantly **reduced** in liver disease, especially in cirrhosis.
- Affects drugs like:
  - Theophylline
  - Diazepam
  - Lidocaine
  - Propranolol

Phase II Reactions (Conjugation)

- Generally, **less affected** than Phase I.
- Drugs like:
  - Lorazepam
  - Oxazepam
  - Temazepam

    are preferred in hepatic impairment due to minimal Phase I metabolism.

Hepatic extraction ratio (E)

- High E drugs (e.g., morphine, propranolol) → **hepatic clearance depends on blood flow**
- Low E drugs (e.g., phenytoin, theophylline) → **hepatic clearance depends on enzyme capacity**

Liver disease can affect both mechanisms by:

- Decreasing hepatic blood flow (e.g., from portal hypertension)
- Reducing enzyme activity

D. Excretion

- **Biliary excretion** may be impaired in cholestatic liver disease.
- Leads to accumulation of drugs like:
  - Rifampin
  - Erythromycin estolate
  - Oral contraceptives
- **Enterohepatic circulation** may be altered, changing the half-life and effectiveness of certain drugs.

Clinical Consequences

- **Prolonged half-life** and **delayed clearance** of drugs
- **Increased risk of toxicity** from accumulation (e.g., sedatives, opioids, benzodiazepines)
- **Altered therapeutic response**
- Difficulty in dosing **narrow therapeutic index drugs** (e.g., warfarin, phenytoin)

Dosage Considerations in Hepatic Disease

General Principles

- Use **lower starting doses**
- Increase **dosing interval** or reduce **maintenance dose**
- Use **drugs with renal clearance**, if appropriate
- Prefer **conjugated drugs** (Phase II metabolism)
- Avoid **prodrugs** that require hepatic activation
- Monitor **clinical response** and **toxicity signs**

Child-Pugh Score

- Used to assess the severity of liver disease and guide dosage adjustments.

Parameter	Score 1	Score 2	Score 3
Bilirubin (mg/dL)	<2	2–3	>3
Albumin (g/dL)	>3.5	2.8–3.5	<2.8
INR	<1.7	1.7–2.3	>2.3
Ascites	None	Mild	Moderate/Severe
Encephalopathy	None	Grade 1–2	Grade 3–4

- **Class A**: Mild (Score 5–6)
- **Class B**: Moderate (7–9)
- **Class C**: Severe (10–15)

Examples of Drug Adjustments in Hepatic Impairment

Drug	Effect in Liver Disease	Adjustment
Diazepam	Reduced metabolism → sedation, coma	Avoid or use alternatives
Propranolol	Increased bioavailability	Use with caution
Morphine	Reduced clearance, increased effect	Reduce dose
Warfarin	Altered protein binding and metabolism	Monitor INR closely
Theophylline	Decreased clearance	Reduce dose, monitor levels
Acetaminophen	Risk of hepatotoxicity	Limit to ≤2 g/day or avoid
Metronidazole	Decreased metabolism	Reduce dose

Summary

PK Process	Effect of Hepatic Disease
Absorption	Decreased in severe liver disease
Distribution	Increased free drug due to low albumin
Metabolism	Decreased (especially Phase I)
Excretion	Impaired biliary elimination

6. Population Pharmacokinetics (PopPK)

- **Population pharmacokinetics (PopPK)** is a branch of pharmacokinetics that studies the variability in drug concentrations across individuals in target populations receiving clinically relevant doses of a drug.
- Unlike classical pharmacokinetics, which often studies a small number of healthy volunteers under controlled conditions.
- PopPK deals with real-world data from diverse patient groups, including those with various diseases, ages, organ functions, and genetic backgrounds.
- PopPK is crucial for optimizing drug dosing, improving therapeutic efficacy, and minimizing toxicity.
- It helps answer how a drug behaves in different patient populations and informs dose adjustments for special groups.

Basic Concepts in Pharmacokinetics

- Before diving into PopPK, it's helpful to understand basic pharmacokinetic parameters:
  - **Absorption** - How a drug enters systemic circulation.
  - **Distribution** - How a drug spreads through body tissues and fluids.
  - **Metabolism** - How the body chemically alters the drug.
  - **Excretion** - How the drug or its metabolites are eliminated.
- Pharmacokinetics is often described by parameters such as:
  - **Clearance (CL)** - Volume of plasma cleared of drug per unit time.
  - **Volume of Distribution (Vd)** - Apparent volume in which a drug is distributed.
  - **Half-life ($t^{1/2}$)** - Time required for drug concentration to reduce by half.
  - **Bioavailability (F)** - Proportion of the drug that enters systemic circulation.

What Is Population Pharmacokinetics?

- Population pharmacokinetics investigates how demographic, pathophysiological, and environmental factors influence drug concentration-time profiles across individuals in a population.
- It uses statistical models to describe variability between individuals (interindividual variability) and within individuals (intraindividual variability).

Objectives

- Identify patient factors that affect drug exposure.
- Quantify variability in pharmacokinetic parameters.
- Optimize dosing regimens for subpopulations.
- Predict drug concentrations in patients with limited data.

Key Components of PopPK Modelling

- **Structural Model**: Describes the typical pharmacokinetics of the drug (e.g., one- or two-compartment models).
- **Statistical Model**: Accounts for random variability:
  - **Interindividual variability (IIV)**: Differences between patients.
  - **Residual variability**: Measurement error or model misspecification.
- **Covariate Model**: Explains variability using measurable patient factors (e.g., weight, age, sex, creatinine clearance).

Data Collection for PopPK

- Data are often collected from **sparse sampling** in a large population rather than rich sampling from a few individuals.
- Data sources can include clinical trials, therapeutic drug monitoring (TDM), and real-world clinical practice.
- PopPK studies may be **prospective** or **retrospective**.

Modelling Methods

Common software/tools

- **NONMEM** (Nonlinear Mixed-Effects Modeling)
- **Monolix**
- **Phoenix NLME**
- **R packages** (e.g., nlme, mrgsolve)

Approaches

- **Nonlinear mixed-effects modeling (NLME)** is the gold standard.
- **Bayesian estimation** and **machine learning** methods are increasingly explored.

Covariate Analysis in PopPK

- Covariates help explain IIV and refine dose recommendations.
- Common covariates include
  - **Demographic**: age, gender, weight, body surface area
  - **Genetic**: polymorphisms in metabolizing enzymes (e.g., CYP450 genes)
  - **Physiological**: renal/hepatic function, disease state
  - **Co-medications**: drug-drug interactions
- Incorporating covariates can lead to **individualized therapy** and **dose adjustment algorithms**.

Applications of Population Pharmacokinetics

- **Drug Development**:
  - Supports dose selection for phase II/III trials
  - Identifies patient subgroups for special consideration
- **Regulatory Submissions**:
  - FDA and EMA encourage PopPK in new drug applications (NDAs)

- **Therapeutic Drug Monitoring (TDM)**:
  - Guides dosing in clinical settings (e.g., antibiotics, antiepileptics)
- **Special Populations**:
  - Dosing in pediatrics, geriatrics, pregnant women, organ-impaired patients
- **Model-Informed Precision Dosing (MIPD)**:
  - Uses PopPK models integrated with Bayesian forecasting to personalize treatment

Advantages of PopPK

- Requires fewer samples per individual
- Suitable for real-world clinical settings
- Allows inclusion of diverse populations
- Enhances understanding of drug behaviour under variable conditions

Challenges and Limitations

- Data quality and completeness
- Complex model development and validation
- Covariate selection may introduce bias
- Regulatory acceptance may require extensive documentation

Recent Trends and Developments

- **Pharmacogenomics**: Integrating genetic data to explain variability.
- **Model-Informed Drug Development (MIDD)**: Using PopPK alongside pharmacodynamics (PK/PD) for comprehensive insight.
- **Artificial Intelligence and Machine Learning**: Enhancing model predictability and automation.
- **Real-World Evidence (RWE)**: PopPK models built from electronic health records and big data.

Introduction to Bayesian Theory

- **Bayesian theory** refers to a framework for updating beliefs or making decisions based on **Bayes' theorem**, which relates prior knowledge to new evidence.
- It is a fundamental concept in probability theory, statistics, and decision-making.
- Bayesian methods contrast with traditional frequentist statistics by interpreting probability as a **degree of belief** rather than a long-run frequency.
- In Bayesian thinking, probability quantifies uncertainty about parameters or hypotheses, and this uncertainty is updated as new data become available.

Historical Background

- Bayesian theory is named after **Thomas Bayes**, an 18th-century English statistician and minister who formulated the original idea (published posthumously in 1763).
- It was later extended and formalized by **Pierre-Simon Laplace**.
- Although Bayesian methods were initially overlooked in favour of frequentist approaches, the advent of powerful computing in the late 20th century revitalized interest in Bayesian statistics, making it widely used in fields such as medicine, machine learning, economics, and engineering.

Bayes' Theorem: The Core Concept

- Bayes' Theorem mathematically expresses how to update the probability of a hypothesis when given new evidence.

$$\text{Posterior} = \frac{\text{Likelihood} \times \text{Prior}}{\text{Evidence}}$$

Formally:

$$P(H|D) = \frac{P(D|H) \cdot P(H)}{P(D)}$$

Where:

- **P(H/D)**: Posterior probability – the updated probability of the hypothesis HH given data DD.
- **P(D/H)**: Likelihood – the probability of observing data DD given hypothesis HH.
- **P(H)**: Prior probability – the initial belief about HH before seeing the data.
- **P(D)**: Marginal likelihood or evidence – the total probability of the data under all possible hypotheses.

Key Components of Bayesian Analysis

a. Prior Distribution

- Represents the initial belief or knowledge about a parameter before data is observed.
- Priors can be
  - **Informative**: Based on previous studies or expert knowledge.
  - **Non-informative or weakly informative**: Vague or flat priors used when limited prior knowledge exists.

b. Likelihood Function

- Describes how likely the observed data is, given different values of the unknown parameter.
- It is derived from the probability model of the data.

c. Posterior Distribution

- The updated belief about the parameter after incorporating new data.
- It combines the prior and the likelihood.

d. Predictive Distribution

- Provides predictions for new observations based on the posterior distribution.

Bayesian vs. Frequentist Approaches

Aspect	Bayesian	Frequentist
Probability Meaning	Degree of belief	Long-run frequency
Parameters	Treated as random variables	Treated as fixed (but unknown)
Inference	Based on posterior distribution	Based on sampling distribution
Confidence Intervals	Credible intervals (Bayesian)	Confidence intervals (Frequentist)
Hypothesis Testing	Bayes factors, posterior probabilities	p-values, null hypothesis testing

Applications of Bayesian Theory

- **Medical Diagnosis**: Updating the probability of disease based on test results.
- **Machine Learning**: Bayesian networks, Gaussian processes, Bayesian neural networks.
- **Drug Development**: Bayesian adaptive clinical trials, dose optimization.
- **Economics and Finance**: Risk modelling, decision theory.
- **Artificial Intelligence**: Probabilistic reasoning, robotics.
- **Forensics**: Evaluating the strength of evidence.

Bayesian Computation

- Analytical solutions to posterior distributions are often complex.
- Computational methods are used

a. Markov Chain Monte Carlo (MCMC)

- A class of algorithms (e.g., Gibbs sampling, Metropolis-Hastings) that generate samples from posterior distributions.

b. Variational Inference

- Approximates the posterior distribution with a simpler distribution by optimizing a cost function.

c. Bayesian Software Tools

- Stan
- JAGS (Just Another Gibbs Sampler)
- BUGS (Bayesian inference Using Gibbs Sampling)
- PyMC (Python)
- brms / rstanarm (R)

Advantages of Bayesian Theory

- Incorporates prior knowledge.
- Naturally handles uncertainty.
- Flexible and intuitive interpretation of results.
- Suitable for complex hierarchical models.
- Continual learning: posterior becomes the new prior for future data.

Challenges and Criticisms

- **Choice of Prior**: Subjective or potentially biased.
- **Computational Complexity**: MCMC can be slow and resource-intensive.
- **Interpretability**: Priors and posteriors may be misunderstood.
- **Regulatory Acceptance**: Less traditionally used in regulatory environments (though this is changing).

Example: Bayesian Coin Toss

- Suppose we toss a coin 10 times and observe 7 heads. We want to infer the probability θ\theta of getting a head.
  - Prior: $\theta \sim$ Beta (1,1) (uniform distribution)
  - Likelihood: Binomial (10,θ)
  - Posterior: $\theta|\text{data} \sim \text{Beta}(1+7,1+3)=\text{Beta}(8,4)$
- This posterior gives the full range of likely values for θ, not just a single point estimate.

- Bayesian theory provides a coherent, flexible, and powerful framework for statistical inference and decision-making under uncertainty.
- Its core idea—updating beliefs in the light of new evidence—mirrors how humans naturally learn and adapt.

- With increasing computational power and accessible software, Bayesian methods are becoming central to modern science, data analysis, and artificial intelligence.

Adaptive Method or Dosing with Feedback

- **Adaptive dosing** (also known as **dosing with feedback**) is a dynamic approach to drug administration in which drug dosages are individualized and adjusted over time based on patient-specific responses.
- Unlike fixed-dose regimens, adaptive methods tailor dosing using feedback from therapeutic drug monitoring (TDM), biomarkers, clinical outcomes, or pharmacokinetic/pharmacodynamic (PK/PD) models.
- This strategy is especially useful for drugs with
  - Narrow therapeutic windows (e.g., vancomycin, tacrolimus)
  - High inter-individual variability
  - Serious dose-related toxicity or subtherapeutic risk

Concept and Rationale

In traditional dosing

- A "one-size-fits-all" dose is used based on average patient characteristics.
- Interpatient variability in drug absorption, metabolism, and elimination is not adequately considered.

In adaptive dosing:

- Initial dosing is based on population data or individualized estimates.
- **Feedback** from observed drug concentrations or clinical outcomes is used to **adjust future doses**.
- The goal is to **optimize therapeutic effect** while **minimizing adverse effects**.

Key Components of Adaptive Dosing

a. Initial Dose Estimation

- Based on population PK models
- Adjusted for known patient-specific covariates (weight, age, renal function)

b. Feedback Collection

- Measured **drug concentrations** (e.g., through TDM)
- **Biomarkers** (e.g., INR for warfarin, HbA1c for insulin therapy)
- **Clinical endpoints** (e.g., blood pressure, symptom relief)

c. Model-Based Dose Adjustment

- Uses feedback to update estimates of individual PK/PD parameters
- Employs **Bayesian forecasting**, machine learning, or regression models
- Provides a new personalized dose

d. Iteration

- The process is **repeated** as more data becomes available

Methods of Adaptive Dosing

a. Empirical Titration

- Based on clinical response or side effects (e.g., increasing insulin if glucose remains high)

b. Therapeutic Drug Monitoring (TDM)

- Adjusting doses based on measured drug levels in blood
- Used for drugs with narrow therapeutic index (e.g., aminoglycosides, antiepileptics)

c. Bayesian Forecasting

- Uses prior population data and individual patient data
- Updates patient-specific PK parameters (e.g., clearance, volume of distribution)
- Predicts future concentrations and recommends optimal dosing

d. Model-Informed Precision Dosing (MIPD)

- Integrates population PK/PD models, patient covariates, and TDM data
- Advanced software platforms support real-time individualized dosing decisions

Bayesian Adaptive Dosing: An Example

Drug: Vancomycin (an antibiotic with nephrotoxicity risk)

- **Step 1**: Start with a population PK model for vancomycin.
- **Step 2**: Measure serum concentration after the first dose (e.g., trough level).
- **Step 3**: Use Bayesian estimation to update the patient's PK parameters.
- **Step 4**: Predict the concentration profile and adjust the next dose to achieve the target AUC (Area Under the Curve).
- **Step 5**: Continue monitoring and adjusting.

This approach maintains therapeutic levels and avoids toxicity.

Advantages of Adaptive Dosing

- **Improved efficacy**: Ensures drug exposure is within therapeutic range.
- **Reduced toxicity**: Minimizes risk of overdose or adverse effects.
- **Personalization**: Tailors treatment to individual PK/PD characteristics.
- **Better outcomes**: Especially in vulnerable populations (e.g., neonates, renal-impaired patients)
- **Real-time optimization**: Can adjust to changing physiology (e.g., disease progression)

Applications in Medicine

Area	Example	Notes
Infectious Diseases	Vancomycin, Aminoglycosides	Target AUC/MIC ratios
Transplant Medicine	Tacrolimus, Cyclosporine	Narrow therapeutic index
Cardiology	Warfarin, Digoxin	Dosing guided by INR or levels
Diabetes	Insulin	Adjusted using glucose levels
Oncology	Chemotherapy (e.g., methotrexate)	Feedback on toxicity and levels
Neurology	Antiepileptics (e.g., phenytoin)	Serum drug levels and seizure control

Challenges and Limitations

- **Data collection**: Requires timely and accurate drug level monitoring.
- **Complexity**: Bayesian or model-based tools need training and validation.
- **Computational requirements**: Advanced models may need specialized software.
- **Uncertain priors**: In Bayesian models, poorly chosen priors can mislead dosing.
- **Implementation cost**: Requires infrastructure and training in clinical settings.

Emerging Trends

- **Artificial Intelligence & Machine Learning**: Real-time dose optimization based on patient data streams.
- **Integration with Electronic Health Records (EHRs)**: Automated alerts and dose recommendations.
- **Closed-Loop Drug Delivery Systems**: Devices (e.g., insulin pumps) that auto-adjust dose based on feedback.
- **Precision Medicine**: Genomic and proteomic data used to inform initial dosing and adjustments.

- Adaptive dosing with feedback represents a shift toward **precision medicine**, where therapy is customized to the individual patient's biology and response.
- By continuously integrating clinical data and drug levels, this method improves treatment safety and effectiveness.
- While implementation challenges remain, advances in computational tools and digital health infrastructure are making adaptive dosing increasingly feasible in routine clinical care.

Analysis of Population Pharmacokinetic (PopPK) Data

- **Population pharmacokinetics (PopPK)** deals with understanding how drugs are absorbed, distributed, metabolized, and excreted (ADME) in various individuals within a target population.
- PopPK analysis focuses on quantifying the variability in drug exposure and identifying covariates (patient characteristics) that explain this variability.
- The **analysis of PopPK data** involves collecting drug concentration data from a diverse patient group, modelling this data using statistical methods (primarily nonlinear mixed-effects modelling), and interpreting the results to guide clinical decision-making and dosing strategies.

Goals of PopPK Data Analysis

- Estimate **typical values** of pharmacokinetic (PK) parameters in a population.
- Quantify **variability** between individuals and within individuals.
- Identify **covariates** that explain inter-individual variability.
- Predict drug concentration-time profiles in individuals or subgroups.
- Optimize and personalize **drug dosing** strategies.

Steps in Population Pharmacokinetic Data Analysis

Step 1: Data Collection and Preparation

a. Sources of Data

- Clinical trials (Phase I–IV)
- Therapeutic drug monitoring (TDM)
- Real-world clinical data (electronic health records)

b. Data Types Required

- **Demographic data**: Age, weight, sex, ethnicity
- **Clinical data**: Creatinine clearance, liver function, disease status
- **Dosing history**: Dose amount, time of administration
- **Concentration data**: Plasma/blood concentrations of the drug
- **Time variables**: Time after dose (TAD), sampling time

c. Data Cleaning

- Handling missing data
- Standardizing units
- Removing outliers or implausible values

Step 2: Model Building

Modelling in PopPK is usually done using **Nonlinear Mixed-Effects Modeling (NLME)**.

a. Software Tools

- **NONMEM** (most widely used)
- **Monolix**
- **Phoenix NLME**
- **Stan, R (nlme, nlmixr), BUGS/JAGS**

b. Structural Model

Defines the PK model that best describes the drug concentration-time profile:

- **One-compartment** or **two-compartment** models
- **First-order absorption, zero-order absorption, lag time**

Common PK parameters:

- Clearance (CL)
- Volume of distribution (Vd)
- Absorption rate constant (Ka)

c. Statistical Model

Describes variability and residual error.

- **Interindividual variability (IIV)**:

$$\theta_i = \theta \cdot e^{\eta_i}$$

- **Residual unexplained variability (RUV)**:

$$C_{obs} = C_{pred} + \varepsilon$$

d. Covariate Model

Incorporates patient-specific variables to explain variability in PK parameters:

- Continuous covariates: weight, age, CrCL
- Categorical covariates: sex, genotype, disease state

Example:

$$CL_i = CL_{typ} \cdot \left(\frac{WT_i}{70} \right)^{0.75} \cdot e^{\eta_i}$$

Step 3: Model Evaluation and Diagnostics

a. Goodness-of-Fit Plots

- Observed vs. predicted concentrations
- Conditional weighted residuals (CWRES) vs. time or predictions

b. Statistical Criteria

- Objective function value (OFV)
- Akaike Information Criterion (AIC), Bayesian Information Criterion (BIC)

c. Visual Predictive Check (VPC)

- Simulates multiple datasets from the model
- Compares observed data with predicted intervals

d. Bootstrap Analysis

- Resampling with replacement to assess parameter uncertainty

e. Normalized Prediction Distribution Errors (NPDE)

- Assesses how well the model predicts the distribution of data

Step 4: Covariate Analysis and Model Refinement

a. Covariate Selection Methods

- Forward inclusion/backward elimination
- Stepwise covariate modeling (SCM)
- Information criteria-based selection

b. Biological Plausibility

- Selected covariates should make pharmacological or clinical sense

c. Final Model

- Includes structural, statistical, and covariate components
- Should be parsimonious (as simple as possible, but still accurate)

Step 5: Model Application and Simulation

a. Simulation of Dosing Regimens

- Predict concentration-time profiles under different dosing scenarios
- Evaluate probability of target attainment (PTA)

b. Bayesian Forecasting

- Uses prior information + patient data to update individual PK estimates
- Informs individualized dosing in real-time

c. Model-Informed Precision Dosing (MIPD)

- Integration of PopPK models into clinical practice
- Used in clinical decision support systems (e.g., InsightRx, TDMx)

Challenges in PopPK Data Analysis

- Sparse data in routine settings
- Missing covariate data
- Model misspecification
- Collinearity among covariates
- Computational complexity for large datasets
- Ethical concerns in model extrapolation to special populations (e.g., paediatrics)

Example Application

Drug: Gentamicin (an aminoglycoside antibiotic)

- **Population**: Hospitalized adults with variable renal function
- **Structural model**: One-compartment, first-order elimination
- **Covariate**: Creatinine clearance significantly affects clearance
- **Outcome**: Final model allows estimation of optimal dose for each patient based on renal function

Regulatory Perspective

Regulatory agencies (e.g., FDA, EMA) encourage PopPK analysis in

- **New drug applications (NDAs)**
- **Labeling recommendations**
- **Post-marketing studies**
- **Special population dosing** (e.g., children, elderly, renal impairment)

➢ Analyzing population pharmacokinetic data is a critical part of modern drug development and personalized medicine.

➢ Through the use of nonlinear mixed-effects modelling and incorporation of patient-specific covariates, PopPK analysis helps in understanding variability in drug response, guiding dosage individualization, and improving clinical outcomes.

➢ Advances in software, computational power, and integration with electronic health systems are further enhancing the role of PopPK in real-world healthcare.

7. Pharmacogenetics

- **Pharmacogenetics** is the branch of pharmacology that studies how genetic variation among individuals influences their response to drugs.
- This field combines principles of pharmacology (the science of drug action) and genetics (the study of genes and heredity) to understand why people respond differently to medications.
- The ultimate goal of pharmacogenetics is to tailor drug therapy to individual genetic profiles, ensuring maximum efficacy and minimal side effects.

Definition and Scope

- **Pharmacogenetics** refers specifically to the study of **single gene variations** and their effects on drug response.
- It is a subset of the broader field of **pharmacogenomics**, which involves the study of **genomic** (entire genome) influences on drug response.

Historical Background

- The concept of pharmacogenetics began in the 1950s when it was observed that some individuals had unusual reactions to standard drug dosages.
- For example,
    - **Primaquine-induced hemolytic anemia** in some African American soldiers was later linked to **G6PD deficiency**.
    - **Prolonged apnea** after succinylcholine administration was found to be due to **butyrylcholinesterase deficiency**.
- These early observations laid the foundation for the development of pharmacogenetics as a scientific field.

Genetic Variations Affecting Drug Response

Genetic differences can affect

- **Drug metabolism**
- **Drug transport**
- **Drug targets (receptors, enzymes)**
- **Immune response to drugs**

a. Drug-Metabolizing Enzymes

- Most pharmacogenetic studies focus on **cytochrome P450 (CYP450)** enzymes, a family of liver enzymes that metabolize many drugs.
- **Key enzymes**
  - **CYP2D6**: Affects metabolism of antidepressants, opioids (e.g., codeine)
  - **CYP2C9**: Involved in metabolism of warfarin, phenytoin
  - **CYP2C19**: Important for drugs like clopidogrel, omeprazole
- **Phenotypes**
  - **Poor metabolizers**: Reduced or absent enzyme activity
  - **Intermediate metabolizers**: Reduced activity
  - **Extensive metabolizers**: Normal activity
  - **Ultra-rapid metabolizers**: Increased activity due to gene duplication

b. Drug Transporters

- **ABCB1 (P-glycoprotein)**: Affects drug absorption and distribution (e.g., digoxin, antiretrovirals)
- **SLCO1B1**: Affects statin transport; variants can lead to increased risk of statin-induced myopathy.

c. Drug Targets

- Genetic polymorphisms in drug targets such as receptors and enzymes can alter drug efficacy:
    - **VKORC1** (Vitamin K epoxide reductase complex subunit 1): Affects warfarin sensitivity.
    - **Beta-adrenergic receptor variants**: May affect response to beta-blockers.

d. Immune Response Genes

- Some gene variants predispose individuals to adverse drug reactions (ADRs):
    - **HLA-B*57:01**: Associated with hypersensitivity to abacavir (HIV treatment)
    - **HLA-B*15:02**: Linked to Stevens-Johnson Syndrome with carbamazepine

Clinical Applications

a. Personalized Medicine

- Pharmacogenetics allows for **precision medicine**—prescribing the right drug at the right dose for the right patient. This improves:
    - Drug efficacy
    - Safety
    - Patient compliance

b. Avoidance of Adverse Drug Reactions

- Pharmacogenetic testing can identify individuals at risk of severe ADRs, such as
    - Warfarin-induced bleeding
    - Severe skin reactions
    - Drug-induced liver injury

c. Optimizing Drug Dosage

- For drugs with narrow therapeutic windows (e.g., warfarin), genetic testing helps in determining the optimal starting dose.

d. Oncology

- In cancer treatment, pharmacogenetics is crucial:
    - Testing for **TPMT** gene before administering thiopurines (e.g., azathioprine)
    - **KRAS/NRAS** status before using EGFR inhibitors in colorectal cancer
    - **HER2** expression in breast cancer (trastuzumab suitability)

Pharmacogenetic Testing

a. Sample Collection

- Typically involves a buccal swab or blood sample.

b. Methods

- PCR (Polymerase Chain Reaction)
- DNA sequencing
- Microarray analysis

c. Commercial Tests

Several FDA-approved pharmacogenetic tests are available for drugs like

- Clopidogrel
- Warfarin
- Abacavir
- Irinotecan

Challenges and Limitations

- **Complexity of drug response**: Influenced by multiple genes and environmental factors.
- **Lack of awareness among clinicians**
- **Cost and accessibility** of testing
- **Ethical concerns**: Privacy, genetic discrimination
- **Regulatory issues**: Need for standardized guidelines

Future Prospects

- Integration with **electronic health records (EHRs)** to guide prescriptions in real-time.
- Development of **multi-gene panels** to predict drug response.
- Wider use in **psychiatry, cardiology, infectious diseases**, and beyond.
- Progress in **AI and bioinformatics** will accelerate the translation of genetic data into clinical decisions.

- ➢ Pharmacogenetics represents a transformative approach to drug therapy.
- ➢ By understanding the genetic makeup of individuals, healthcare providers can predict how a person will respond to a medication, thus enabling safer, more effective, and personalized treatments.
- ➢ As the cost of genetic testing decreases and awareness grows, pharmacogenetics is poised to become a cornerstone of modern medicine.

Genetic Polymorphism in Drug Metabolism: Cytochrome P-450 Isoenzymes

- Drug metabolism refers to the biochemical modification of pharmaceutical substances by living organisms, primarily through specialized enzymatic systems.
- The liver is the principal organ for drug metabolism, with the **Cytochrome P450 (CYP450)** family of enzymes playing a central role.
- Genetic polymorphisms—naturally occurring variations in DNA sequences among individuals—significantly influence the activity of these enzymes, leading to variability in drug response, efficacy, and risk of adverse effects.

Types of Genetic Polymorphisms

The most common types of polymorphisms affecting drug metabolism include

- **Single Nucleotide Polymorphisms (SNPs)**
  - ➢ Substitution of a single base pair in the DNA sequence.
  - ➢ Can result in:
    - ▪ Silent mutations (no change in protein)
    - ▪ Missense mutations (altered amino acid)
    - ▪ Nonsense mutations (premature stop codon)
- **Insertions/Deletions (Indels)**
  - ➢ Addition or deletion of small DNA fragments.
  - ➢ Can lead to frameshifts or altered protein expression.
- **Copy Number Variations (CNVs)**
  - ➢ Duplications or deletions of entire genes.
  - ➢ Can lead to increased (e.g., gene duplications) or null enzyme activity (e.g., gene deletions).

Phenotypes Associated with Metabolic Capacity

Phenotype	Enzyme Activity	Clinical Relevance
Poor Metabolizer (PM)	Little to no activity	Increased risk of toxicity or therapeutic failure
Intermediate Metabolizer (IM)	Reduced activity	May need dose adjustment
Extensive Metabolizer (EM)	Normal activity	Expected therapeutic response
Ultra-Rapid Metabolizer (UM)	Increased activity	Subtherapeutic response due to rapid clearance or fast activation

Overview of Cytochrome P450 Enzymes

- Cytochrome P450 enzymes are a superfamily of heme-containing monooxygenases.
- They are responsible for the oxidative metabolism of a wide range of endogenous compounds (e.g., steroids, fatty acids) and xenobiotics, including drugs, environmental chemicals, and toxins.
- In humans, about 57 functional CYP genes have been identified, grouped into families and subfamilies based on sequence homology.
- The most clinically important CYP450 isoenzymes involved in drug metabolism include:
    - **CYP3A4/5**
    - **CYP2D6**
    - **CYP2C9**
    - **CYP2C19**
    - **CYP1A2**
    - **CYP2E1**

Genetic Polymorphism and Its Implications

- Genetic polymorphisms in CYP genes can lead to **functional variability**, which affects the metabolic capacity of individuals.
- Based on enzyme activity, individuals are generally classified into four phenotypes
    - **Poor Metabolizers (PM):** Little or no functional enzyme activity.
    - **Intermediate Metabolizers (IM):** Reduced enzyme activity.
    - **Extensive Metabolizers (EM):** Normal enzyme activity.
    - **Ultra-Rapid Metabolizers (UM):** Increased enzyme activity due to gene duplication or other mechanisms.
- These phenotypes have significant implications in clinical pharmacology, influencing:
    - **Drug efficacy**
    - **Toxicity and side effects**
    - **Dosage requirements**
    - **Drug–drug interactions**

CYP2D6 Polymorphism

- **Substrates:** Antidepressants, antipsychotics, beta-blockers, opioids (codeine, tramadol), tamoxifen.
- **Genetic Variability:**
    - Over 100 allelic variants (e.g., *CYP2D6* *1, *3, *4, *5, *10, *17, *41*).
    - Gene duplication (*CYP2D6*xN) leads to UM phenotype.
    - *CYP2D6 4* is a common null allele in Caucasians.
- **Clinical Impact:**
    - PMs may experience toxicity from standard doses (e.g., nortriptyline).
    - UMs may have subtherapeutic effects due to rapid drug clearance or increased activation of prodrugs (e.g., codeine → morphine conversion).

CYP2C9 Polymorphism

- **Substrates:** Warfarin, phenytoin, NSAIDs, tolbutamide.
- **Common Alleles:** *CYP2C9* *2, *3* (reduced enzyme activity).
- **Clinical Impact:**
  - PMs are at increased risk of bleeding with warfarin due to reduced clearance.
  - Genotyping helps tailor warfarin dosing (along with VKORC1 gene variants).

CYP2C19 Polymorphism

- **Substrates:** Proton pump inhibitors (omeprazole), clopidogrel, diazepam.
- **Common Variants:**
  - *CYP2C19* *2, *3* (non-functional).
  - *CYP2C19 17* (gain-of-function).
- **Clinical Impact:**
  - PMs may have increased efficacy/toxicity with PPIs.
  - Clopidogrel, a prodrug, requires activation by CYP2C19—PMs may have reduced antiplatelet effects, leading to risk of cardiovascular events.
  - UMs may require higher doses for efficacy.

CYP3A4/5 Polymorphism

- **Substrates:** Midazolam, cyclosporine, tacrolimus, statins.
- **CYP3A4:**
  - Polymorphisms less frequent, but expression can vary due to environmental and regulatory factors.
- **CYP3A5:**
  - Expressed in some individuals (*CYP3A5 1*), not in others (*CYP3A5 3*).

- **Clinical Impact:**
  - CYP3A5 expressors may metabolize tacrolimus more rapidly, requiring dose adjustment.

CYP1A2 and CYP2E1 Polymorphisms

- **CYP1A2:** Involved in metabolism of caffeine, theophylline, and some antipsychotics. Polymorphisms may affect inducibility.
- **CYP2E1:** Important for metabolizing ethanol, acetaminophen, and small organic molecules. Genetic variants affect susceptibility to drug-induced liver injury.

Non-CYP Enzymes

a. N-Acetyltransferase (NAT2)

- Metabolizes isoniazid, hydralazine, sulfonamides.
- Two phenotypes: slow and fast acetylators.
- Slow acetylators (common in Europeans) are at risk of isoniazid-induced hepatotoxicity.

b. Thiopurine S-methyltransferase (TPMT)

- Metabolizes thiopurine drugs (azathioprine, mercaptopurine).
- TPMT*2, *3A, *3C → reduced activity.
- PMs risk severe myelosuppression if standard doses are used.

c. UDP-Glucuronosyltransferases (UGTs)

- Metabolize bilirubin, morphine.
- UGT1A1*28 variant causes Gilbert's syndrome.
- Affects metabolism of irinotecan → increased toxicity in PMs.

Clinical and Pharmacogenomic Applications

- **Personalized Medicine:**
  - Pharmacogenetic testing enables individualized drug therapy based on CYP450 genotype.
  - Avoids trial-and-error prescribing, enhances efficacy, and reduces adverse effects.
- **Therapeutic Drug Monitoring (TDM):**
  - Useful when polymorphism leads to variable drug concentrations (e.g., phenytoin, warfarin).
- **Regulatory Guidance:**
  - Agencies like the FDA recommend pharmacogenetic labeling for drugs metabolized by polymorphic CYP enzymes.
- **Drug Efficacy and Safety**
  - PMs may accumulate drugs to toxic levels.
  - UMs may eliminate drugs too rapidly, reducing efficacy.
- **Personalized Dosing**
  - Genotype-guided dosing improves therapeutic outcomes.
  - Example: Warfarin dosing based on CYP2C9 and VKORC1 genotypes.
- **Drug Development**
  - Pharmacogenetics aids in designing safer and more effective drugs.
  - Stratifying patients in clinical trials based on metabolic capacity.
- **Adverse Drug Reactions (ADRs)**
  - Many ADRs can be traced to poor metabolizer phenotypes.
  - Genotyping can prevent life-threatening toxicity.

Challenges and Considerations

- **Ethnic variability:** Allele frequencies differ across populations, affecting generalizability.
- **Environmental factors:** Diet, smoking, comorbidities, and co-medications can modulate enzyme activity.
- **Polygenic effects:** Drug response often influenced by multiple genes beyond CYPs (e.g., transporters, receptors).

➢ Genetic polymorphisms in cytochrome P-450 isoenzymes are a major determinant of interindividual variability in drug metabolism.

➢ Understanding these variations is essential for optimizing pharmacotherapy and achieving the goals of personalized medicine.

➢ With increasing availability of pharmacogenomic tools and growing clinical awareness, CYP450 genotyping is becoming a key component in tailoring safe and effective drug regimens.

Genetic Polymorphism in Drug Transport and Drug Targets

- Drug response in individuals is influenced not only by differences in drug-metabolizing enzymes but also by variations in **drug transporters** and **drug targets**.
- These genetic differences, collectively referred to as **pharmacogenomic polymorphisms**, can alter the **absorption, distribution, efficacy, and toxicity** of therapeutic agents.
- Understanding these genetic polymorphisms is crucial for advancing **personalized medicine**, improving drug efficacy, and minimizing adverse drug reactions.

Genetic Polymorphism in Drug Transport

- Drug transporters are membrane proteins that regulate the movement of drugs across cellular membranes, affecting their absorption (especially in the intestines), distribution (e.g., to the brain or liver), and excretion (e.g., through bile or urine).
- These transporters are broadly classified into two families:
  - **ATP-binding cassette (ABC) transporters** – Mediate **efflux** of drugs out of cells.
  - **Solute carrier (SLC) transporters** – Facilitate **uptake** of drugs into cells.
- Genetic polymorphisms in these transporters can significantly impact drug bioavailability and therapeutic outcome.

ABC Transporters

a. ABCB1 (MDR1, P-glycoprotein)

- **Function:** Efflux transporter that pumps drugs out of cells (e.g., intestinal epithelium, blood-brain barrier).
- **Substrates:** Digoxin, cyclosporine, tacrolimus, antiretrovirals, chemotherapeutics.
- **Common Polymorphisms:**
  - **C3435T (rs1045642)** – Associated with reduced protein expression.
  - **G2677T/A (rs2032582)** – Alters substrate specificity.
- **Clinical Impact:**
  - Polymorphisms can affect drug absorption and resistance.
  - Example: Variants associated with altered plasma levels of digoxin and resistance to chemotherapy.

b. ABCC2 (MRP2)

- **Function:** Efflux of drugs and conjugated metabolites.
- **Substrates:** Methotrexate, irinotecan, antiretrovirals.
- **Polymorphisms:**
  - **-24C>T (rs717620)** – Affects drug clearance.
- **Impact:** Reduced transporter function may increase systemic drug exposure and toxicity.

c. ABCG2 (BCRP)

- **Function:** Efflux transporter at intestinal, hepatic, and placental barriers.
- **Substrates:** Anticancer drugs (e.g., topotecan, imatinib), sulfasalazine.
- **Polymorphism:**
  - **421C>A (Q141K, rs2231142)** – Decreases protein stability and efflux activity.
- **Clinical Impact:** Increased bioavailability and drug toxicity in variant carriers.

SLC Transporters

a. SLCO1B1 (OATP1B1)

- **Function:** Hepatic uptake of statins, methotrexate, and other drugs.
- **Polymorphism:**
  - **521T>C (Val174Ala, rs4149056)** – Reduces transporter activity.
- **Clinical Impact:**
  - Associated with increased plasma levels of simvastatin and higher risk of **statin-induced myopathy**.
  - FDA recommends dose adjustments or alternative drugs based on genotype.

b. SLC22A1 (OCT1)

- **Function:** Hepatic uptake of organic cations, including metformin.
- **Polymorphisms:**
  - Several loss-of-function variants affect drug uptake.
- **Clinical Impact:**
  - Affects metformin efficacy in type 2 diabetes.

c. SLC6A4 (Serotonin transporter - SERT)

- **Function:** Reuptake of serotonin in neurons.
- **Polymorphisms:**
  - **5-HTTLPR (promoter region)** - Short ("S") and long ("L") alleles.
- **Clinical Impact:**
  - S allele associated with lower expression, affecting response to SSRIs (e.g., fluoxetine).
  - Linked to increased risk of depression and anxiety disorders.

Genetic Polymorphism in Drug Targets

- Drug targets include receptors, enzymes, ion channels, and other proteins that drugs bind to in order to exert their effects.
- Genetic variation in these targets can affect **drug binding affinity**, **signal transduction**, and **clinical efficacy or toxicity**.

Receptors

a. ADRB1 and ADRB2 (Beta-adrenergic receptors)

- **Target Drugs:** Beta-blockers (e.g., metoprolol), beta-agonists (e.g., salbutamol).
- **Polymorphisms:**
  - **ADRB1 Arg389Gly** – Alters response to beta-blockers.
  - **ADRB2 Gly16Arg, Gln27Glu** – Associated with variable bronchodilator response.
- **Clinical Impact:**
  - Certain genotypes may require adjusted dosing or alternative therapy in asthma or heart failure.

b. DRD2 (Dopamine D2 receptor)

- **Target Drugs:** Antipsychotics, such as risperidone and haloperidol.
- **Polymorphisms:**
  - **Taq1A (rs1800497)** – Affects receptor density.
- **Clinical Impact:** May influence treatment response and risk of extrapyramidal side effects.

Enzymes

a. VKORC1 (Vitamin K epoxide reductase complex subunit 1)

- **Target Drug:** Warfarin.
- **Polymorphism:**
  - **-1639G>A (rs9923231)** – Alters gene expression.
- **Clinical Impact:**
  - Individuals with AA genotype require lower warfarin doses.
  - Combined genotyping of VKORC1 and CYP2C9 used to predict optimal dosing.

b. HMGCR (HMG-CoA reductase)

- **Target Drug:** Statins.
- **Polymorphisms:**
    - Associated with variability in cholesterol-lowering response.
- **Clinical Impact:** Some variants show reduced LDL-C reduction despite statin therapy.

Ion Channels

a. KCNH2 (HERG gene)

- **Target:** Cardiac potassium channel.
- **Relevance:** Drug-induced long QT syndrome (e.g., with certain antiarrhythmics, antibiotics).
- **Polymorphisms:** Variants may predispose to QT prolongation and torsades de pointes.
- **Clinical Impact:** Genotyping may guide safer drug selection in susceptible individuals.

Clinical Relevance of Genetic Polymorphisms in Drug Transport and Targets

Aspect	Impact of Genetic Polymorphism
Drug Absorption	ABC transporter variants can alter oral bioavailability.
Drug Distribution	Polymorphisms affect tissue penetration (e.g., blood-brain barrier).
Drug Efficacy	Target receptor or enzyme polymorphisms can enhance or diminish drug response.
Adverse Effects	Transporter and target variants may lead to increased toxicity or therapeutic failure.
Personalized Medicine	Pharmacogenetic testing allows dose optimization and drug selection.

Examples of Clinically Relevant Gene–Drug Pairs

Gene	Drug	Clinical Implication
SLCO1B1	Simvastatin	Risk of myopathy; dose adjustment recommended
ABCB1	Digoxin	Altered plasma levels and potential toxicity
VKORC1	Warfarin	Genotype-guided dosing to prevent bleeding
SLC6A4	SSRIs	Affects antidepressant efficacy
ADRB2	Salbutamol	Variable bronchodilator response in asthma
OCT1	Metformin	Altered efficacy in glycemic control

Challenges and Future Directions

- **Population Diversity:** Allele frequencies vary among ethnic groups.
- **Clinical Implementation:** Need for cost-effective, accessible genotyping.
- **Gene–Environment Interactions:** Diet, lifestyle, and comorbidities may influence expression.
- **Regulatory and Ethical Concerns:** Use of genetic data must ensure patient privacy and informed consent.

Pharmacogenetics and Pharmacokinetics/Pharmacodynamic Considerations

- Pharmacogenetics is the study of how genetic variations influence an individual's response to drugs.
- It is a subfield of **pharmacogenomics**, focusing specifically on **single gene variations** that affect drug action.
- Pharmacogenetics is critically important in understanding and optimizing drug therapy, particularly in terms of **pharmacokinetics (PK)** and **pharmacodynamics (PD)**.

- Understanding these interactions allows for the development of **personalized medicine**, aiming to tailor drug therapy based on individual genetic profiles to improve efficacy and reduce adverse drug reactions.

Pharmacokinetics (PK): Definition and Genetic Considerations

Definition: Pharmacokinetics describes **what the body does to a drug**, encompassing four primary processes:

- **Absorption**
- **Distribution**
- **Metabolism**
- **Excretion**

Genetic Impact on PK:

a. Absorption

- **Transporters** in the gut wall (e.g., ABCB1, SLCO1B1) affect drug uptake.
- Polymorphisms in these genes can **increase or decrease bioavailability**.

b. Distribution

- Variants in genes encoding plasma proteins (e.g., **alpha-1 acid glycoprotein, albumin**) or transporters (e.g., **ABCG2**) influence drug distribution in tissues.
- Affects drug availability at the target site.

c. Metabolism

- The most extensively studied area in pharmacogenetics.
- Polymorphisms in genes encoding **cytochrome P450 enzymes** (CYP2D6, CYP2C9, CYP2C19) drastically affect drug metabolism rates.

Metabolizer status

Phenotype	Metabolic Activity
Poor Metabolizer (PM)	Little to no enzyme activity
Intermediate Metabolizer (IM)	Reduced activity
Extensive Metabolizer (EM)	Normal activity
Ultra-Rapid Metabolizer (UM)	Increased activity (e.g., gene duplications)

d. Excretion

- Genes encoding renal transporters (e.g., **SLC22A2, ABCG2**) affect renal drug clearance.
- Altered excretion can lead to drug accumulation and toxicity.

Pharmacodynamics (PD): Definition and Genetic Considerations

Definition: Pharmacodynamics refers to **what the drug does to the body**, including:

- **Mechanism of action**
- **Drug–receptor interactions**
- **Signal transduction**
- **Biological response**

Genetic Impact on PD

a. Drug Targets

- Polymorphisms in drug target genes (e.g., receptors, enzymes, ion channels) can alter **drug binding affinity**, **efficacy**, or **toxicity**.

Examples:

- **VKORC1** polymorphisms affect warfarin sensitivity.
- **ADRB1/ADRB2** variants influence beta-blocker or bronchodilator response.
- **HMGCR** variants can alter statin response.

b. Signal Transduction Pathways

- Genetic variation in intracellular signaling proteins can change the magnitude of the response even when drug-receptor binding is normal.

c. Downstream Effectors

- Genes encoding effector proteins or metabolic pathways involved in the therapeutic effect can modify clinical outcomes.

Interplay Between Pharmacogenetics, PK, and PD

Genetic Variation	Affected Process	Clinical Impact
CYP2C9 polymorphism	Metabolism (PK)	Slower warfarin clearance, bleeding risk
ABCB1 C3435T	Absorption (PK)	Altered bioavailability of digoxin
VKORC1 -1639G>A	Drug target (PD)	Increased warfarin sensitivity
ADRB2 Gly16Arg	Receptor (PD)	Variable bronchodilator response
SLCO1B1 521T>C	Hepatic uptake (PK)	Statin-induced myopathy risk

Clinical Applications of Pharmacogenetic-PK/PD Knowledge

a. Personalized Dosing

- Genetic data can guide initial dosing.
- Example: **Warfarin dosing algorithms** using VKORC1 and CYP2C9 genotypes.

b. Drug Selection

- Avoid drugs that are poorly metabolized or highly toxic in individuals with certain genotypes.
- Example: Avoid **codeine** in CYP2D6 UMs (risk of morphine toxicity) and PMs (ineffective).

c. Predicting Adverse Drug Reactions (ADRs)

- Reduce risk of severe side effects.
- Example: **TPMT genotyping** before thiopurine therapy to prevent myelosuppression.

d. Enhancing Drug Development

- Genetic stratification in clinical trials improves understanding of drug response variability.

Challenges in Clinical Implementation

- **Complex Gene–Drug Interactions:** Multiple genes may influence PK/PD.
- **Ethnic Diversity:** Allele frequencies vary among populations.
- **Cost and Accessibility:** Genetic testing is not yet routine everywhere.
- **Regulatory and Ethical Issues:** Need for guidelines and patient privacy.
- **Physician Education:** Requires training to interpret and apply pharmacogenetic data.

Future Directions

- **Integration into Electronic Health Records (EHRs):** To support clinical decision-making.
- **Pharmacogenomic Panels:** Broader testing covering multiple genes.
- **Population-Specific Guidelines:** Tailored based on genetic diversity.
- **AI and Machine Learning:** For predicting complex gene–drug interactions and guiding therapy.

www.ingramcontent.com/pod-product-compliance
Ingram Content Group UK Ltd.
Pitfield, Milton Keynes, MK11 3LW, UK
UKHW062008290726
14090UKWH00022B/1444

9 798899 611216